OECD Reviews on Local Job Creation

Employment and Skills Strategies in Sweden

Please cite this publication as:
OECD (2015), *Employment and Skills Strategies in Sweden*, OECD Reviews on Local Job Creation, OECD Publishing, Paris.
http://dx.doi.org/10.1787/9789264228641-en

ISBN 978-92-64-22863-4 (print)
ISBN 978-92-64-22864-1 (PDF)

Series: OECD Reviews on Local Job Creation
ISSN 2311-2328 (print)
ISSN 2311-2336 (online)

Photo credits: © Andy Dean Photography/Shutterstock.com; © LalithHerath/Shutterstock.com.

Corrigenda to OECD publications may be found on line at: *www.oecd.org/publishing/corrigenda*.

Preface

Across the OECD, policy-makers are grappling with a critical question: how to create jobs? The recent financial crisis and economic downturn has had serious consequences across most OECD countries, with rising unemployment rates and jobs being lost across many sectors. Indeed, for some countries, the effects the downturn brought with it are continuing, if not amplifying. Shrinking public budgets in some countries also mean that policy makers must now do more with less. In this context, it is necessary to think laterally about how actions in one area, such as employment and training, can have simultaneous benefits in others, such as creating new jobs and better supporting labour market inclusion.

Over recent years, the work of the OECD LEED Programme on *Designing Local Skills Strategies*, *Building Flexibility and Accountability into Local Employment Services*, *Breaking out of Policy Silos*, *Leveraging Training and Skills Development in SMEs*, and *Skills for Competitiveness* has demonstrated that local strategies to boost skills and job creation require the participation of many different actors across employment, training, economic development, and social welfare portfolios. Employers, unions and the non-profit sector are also key partners in ensuring that education and training programmes provide the skills needed in the labour markets of today and the future.

The *OECD Reviews on Local Job Creation* deliver evidence-based and practical recommendations on how to better support employment and economic development at the local level. This report builds on sub-national data analysis and consultations at the national level and with local stakeholders in two case study areas. It provides a comparative framework to understand the role of the local level in contributing to more and better quality jobs. The report can help national, regional and local policy makers in Sweden build effective and sustainable partnerships at the local level, which join-up efforts and achieve stronger outcomes across employment, training, and economic development policies. Co-ordinated policies can help workers find suitable jobs, while also stimulating entrepreneurship and productivity, which increases the quality of life and prosperity within a community as well as throughout the country.

I would like to warmly thank *Arbetsförmedlingen* for their active participation and support of the study.

Sergio Arzeni,
Director, OECD Centre for Entrepreneurship,
SMEs and Local Development

Acknowledgments

This review has been written by the Local Economic and Employment Development (LEED) Programme of the Organisation for Economic Co-operation and Development (OECD) as part of a project undertaken in co-operation with *Arbetsförmedlingen*. This project is part of the OECD LEED programme of work under the leadership of Sylvain Giguère.

The principal authors are Lars Niklasson (Linköping University) and Jonathan Barr, Policy Analyst, OECD. The authors would like to thank Francesca Froy, Senior Policy Analyst, who provided valuable comments on the report. Thanks also go to Michela Meghnagi, and Nikolett Kis for their work on the data analysis, as well as Elisa Campestrin, François Iglesias, Malika Taberkane and other colleagues in the OECD LEED Programme for their assistance with this report.

The authors would also like to acknowledge the valuable contributions of Prof. Dr Gerhard Bosch (University of Duisburg-Essen) for his participation on the project study visit and on-going contributions to this report.

Finally, special thanks are given to the national and local representatives who participated in the project interviews and roundtables, and provided documentation and comments critical to the production of the report.

Table of contents

Tables

Figures

Executive summary

While Sweden weathered the impacts of the economic crisis better than most OECD countries, disparities are rising across the country. Unemployment remains stubbornly high compared to previous national trends and a number of groups, such as immigrants and youth face significant challenges in building labour market success. Creating quality jobs will be a key route towards building new economic advantage and opportunities.

The OECD Local Economic and Employment Development (LEED) programme has developed its reviews on Local Job Creation as an international cross-comparative study examining the contribution of local labour market policy to boosting quality employment and productivity. The review in Sweden has focused on local activities in Gavle and Stockholm. Both regions face unique but inter-connected employment and skills challenges.

This review has analysed how much flexibility local employment and training agencies have in the management of their policies and programmes. *Arbetsförmedlingen* offices (e.g. public employment services) operate within a national framework, which emphasises mobility between regions to reduce overall skills shortages. Activities are tracked and reported through a robust performance and budget management system. While some local offices have taken innovative approaches to tackling unemployment, actions depend on organisational leadership at the local level.

Partnerships will be a key governance tool in Sweden to bring together the comprehensive range of actors involved in employment, skills, and economic development policies. While there is a lot of organised co-operation at the local level, the low flexibility for local *Arbetsförmedlingen* offices influences the nature of collaboration as stakeholders have limited ability to join up their activities to promote growth and employment. Going forward, there is an opportunity to strengthen policy integration through stronger horizontal governance arrangements. For example, while there is a lot of work at the local level to reach people who have a weak position in the labour market, employment policies also need to be better connected to social welfare programmes to ensure those further away receive the necessary income and employment counselling to find a job.

Education and training opportunities play a critical role in building the supply of skills. Sweden has a well-educated population and a high level of skills relative to other OECD countries. As in many other countries, the challenge is how to better connect the education system to the labour market to ensure that the skills being produced are being effectively utilised by employers. The programme of higher vocational education (called *Yrkeshögskolan*) appears to be an innovative and flexible model, which involves employers and includes a workplace training component. Individuals will need to access the education system throughout their lifetime; therefore it is important that flexible part-time learning opportunities are also introduced within the higher vocational education system.

Employer engagement at the local level can help to improve the linkages between the education system and the world of work. Social partners within Sweden, such as unions, have a critical role to play in ensuring that training opportunities build good generic skills, which make people adaptable over their career. Sweden could explore the potential of using career pathways models, which better outline the knowledge, skills, and competencies required for a job and provide a well-articulated transition from education to the labour market. There are experiences in other OECD countries, such as the United States which could serve as useful learning models.

Growth and productivity will become increasingly dependent on making better use of the existing skills of the workforce. In Sweden, there is an opportunity for the public sector to take a stronger leadership role in working with employers to look at their management and human resources practices to ensure they are taking full advantage of their workforce. In other OECD countries, these approaches often involve job redesign and sharing practices and have led to greater profitability and export opportunities when done well.

To build inclusive growth, Sweden has introduced a number of targeted employment and training programmes for those at-risk, including for immigrants and youth who face particular labour market challenges. Local area-based partnerships can play a critical role in developing counselling, mentorship, skills development, work-based training and employment opportunities for these groups, who will be an important source of future competitive advantage.

Key recommendations

Better aligning programmes and policies to local economic development

- Ensure better policy integration and coherence between employment, skills, and economic development actors by strengthening strategic governance structures at the local and regional level.
- Transform regional partnerships into systems of learning which effectively promote evidence-based approaches to job creation, employment, and participation.

Adding value through skills

- Ensure the adult education training system provides flexible opportunities for all individuals to ensure employed individuals can upgrade their skills.
- Increase the engagement of employers (especially SMEs) with the employment and skills system through greater outreach efforts and targeted programmes.
- Better link the supply and demand of skills through the use of career pathways/cluster models.

Targeting policy to local employment sectors and investing in quality jobs

- Emphasise the importance of better utilising skills within employment and training policies and consider the mandate of vocational education institutions to be more proactive in this area.
- Consider the strategic use of public procurement in tackling disadvantage and promoting inclusive growth.

Being inclusive

- Continue to target employment and skills programmes to at-risk youth to develop their employability skills and better connect them with the labour market.

Reader's guide

The *Local Job Creation* project involves a series of country reviews in Australia, Belgium (Flanders), Canada (Ontario and Quebec), Czech Republic, France, Ireland, Israel, Italy (Autonomous Province of Trento), Korea, Sweden, the United Kingdom and the United States (California and Michigan). The key stages of each review are summarised in Box 1.

Box 1. **Summary of the OECD LEED Local Job Creation Project Methodology**

- Analyse available data to understand the key labour market challenges facing the country in the context of the economic recovery and apply an OECD LEED diagnostic tool which seeks to assess the balance between the supply and demand for skills at the local level.
- Map the current policy framework for local job creation in the country.
- Apply the Local Job Creation Dashboard, developed by the OECD LEED Programme (Froy et al., 2010) to measure the relative strengths and weaknesses of local employment and training agencies to contribute to job creation.
- Conduct an OECD study visit, where local and national roundtables with a diverse range of stakeholders are held to discuss the results and refine the findings and recommendations.
- Contribute to policy development in the reviewed country by proposing policy options to overcome barriers, illustrated by selected good practice initiatives from other OECD countries.

While the economic crisis is the current focus of policy-makers, there is a need for both short-term and longer-term actions to ensure sustainable economic growth. In response to this issue, the OECD LEED Programme has developed a set of thematic areas on which employment and training agencies can focus to build sustainable growth at the local level. These include:

1. **Better aligning policies and programmes to local economic development challenges and opportunities;**
2. **Adding value through skills:** Creating an adaptable skilled labour force and supporting employment progression and skills upgrading;
3. **Targeting policy to local employment sectors and investing in quality jobs**, including gearing education and training to emerging local growth sectors and responding to global trends, while working with employers on skills utilisation and productivity; and,
4. **Being inclusive** to ensure that all actual and potential members of the labour force can contribute to future economic growth.

Local Job Creation Dashboard

As part of the OECD Reviews on Local Job Creation, the LEED Programme has drawn on its previous research to develop a set of best practice priorities in each thematic area, which is used to assess local practice through the Local Job Creation Dashboard (see Box 2). The dashboard enables national and local policy-makers to gain a stronger overview of the strengths and weaknesses of the current policy framework, whilst better prioritising future actions and resources. A value between 1 (low) to 5 (high) is assigned to each of the four priority areas corresponding to the relative strengths and weaknesses of local policy approaches based on LEED research and best practices in other OECD countries.

Box 2. **Local Job Creation Dashboard**

Better aligning policies and programmes to local economic development

1.1. Flexibility in the delivery of employment and vocational training policies

1.2. Capacities within employment and VET sectors

1.3. Policy co-ordination, policy integration and co-operation with other sectors

1.4. Evidence based policy making

Adding value through skills

2.1. Flexible training open to all in a broad range of sectors

2.2. Working with employers on training

2.3. Matching people to jobs and facilitating progression

2.4. Joined up approaches to skills

Targeting policy to local employment sectors and investing in quality jobs

3.1. Relevance of provision to important local employment sectors and global trends and challenges

3.2. Working with employers on skills utilisation and productivity

3.3. Promotion of skills for entrepreneurship

3.4. Promoting quality jobs through local economic development

Being inclusive

4.1. Employment and training programmes geared to local "at-risk" groups

4.2. Childcare and family friendly policies to support women's participation in employment

4.3. Tackling youth unemployment

4.4. Openness to immigration

The approach for Sweden

The focus of this study is on the range of policies which boost employment, skills, and economic development. The purpose of the study is to describe and evaluate the effectiveness of these policies, in relation to similar policies across the OECD. The methodology of the study is given by an analytical framework developed by the OECD and applied across a range of countries.

In-depth work was undertaken into two local case studies (Stockholm and Gävle) to understand the implementation of these policies. The study uses statistics to assess the levels of skills and unemployment in the case study regions. Interviews were undertaken with stakeholders in each region through group discussions and individual interviews (both in person and through email and phone). Each group consisted of representatives of the employment service (*Arbetsförmedlingen*), skills and training organisations, regional development agencies, local governments and social partners.

The OECD conducted a study visit to Sweden in February 2014 to meet with local and national officials to discuss the preliminary results and findings of the review as well as potential recommendations to improve the overall framework support quality job creation and productivity.

References

Froy, F., S. Giguère and E. Travkina (2010), *Local Job Creation: Project Methodology*, *www.oecd.org/employment/leed/Local%20Job%20Creation%20Methodology_27%20February.pdf.*

Chapter 1

Policy context for employment and skills in Sweden

This chapter provides an overview of Sweden's employment and skills system. Sweden is known for its long tradition of active labour market policy, where the unemployed are offered relatively generous benefits and training opportunities. A key feature of Swedish employment policy is that it has an explicitly national perspective on the labour market. It emphasizes mobility over retraining for the local labour market, meaning that labour market policy operates with a national perspective on the matching of the supply and demand of skills.

The Swedish economy and policies for employment and growth

Sweden is a member state of the European Union, located in the north of Europe next to Denmark, Norway and Finland. The population of 9.6 million is concentrated in the industrialised southern part of Sweden, while the north consists of vast areas of wilderness, populated mainly along the coast, which means that there are strong regional dynamics that need to be taken into account when developing job creation strategies.

Sweden has a large number of successful multi-national companies, a well-developed public sector and high levels of education and skills attainment. While Sweden was not as hard hit by the financial crisis as many other OECD countries, structural changes in the economy are evident. Car manufacturing has been restructured, as well as high tech flagships like pharmaceuticals and telecommunication. Resource-based industries like pulp and paper are under downward pressure, which is impacting employment growth.

Previous OECD research has highlighted how Sweden stands out among OECD member countries as a country with a lower level of inequality (Jamet et al., 2013). Sweden is often regarded as a role model for its employment and training policies, as well as for the autonomy of regional and local governments. The Swedish policy framework has undergone significant change over the past two decades due to economic constraints and the on-going pressure to make public policies more effective and efficient. Policies are increasingly co-ordinated within the European Union, under its "economic semester" and the framework of the Europe 2020-strategy. In the latest National Reform Programme (April 2013), the government indicates that unemployment is expected to remain at relatively high levels.

Despite some positive signals, the unemployment rate is around 8% (see Figure 1.1). Similar to other OECD countries, the crisis has disproportionately impacted certain groups of individuals, such as immigrants and youth. The risk of exclusion is particularly significant for these groups with more than a million individuals who are first or second generation immigrants, living mainly in the big cities. The government projects unemployment to peak at 8.5% in 2014 (Prime Minister's Office, 2013). The official figure for unemployment among youth (between 15-24) was slightly above 22% in December 2012, about half of which are full-time students who have sought employment (see Figure 1.2). However, there are national peculiarities which makes this figure higher in Sweden than in other countries (see Chapter 3 for more information).

It is estimated that 12.7% of the workforce are at the risk of poverty and exclusion, measured as the proportion of 20-64 year-olds who are not in the labour force (or in full time study), long-term unemployed or on long-term sick leave (Prime Minister's Office, 2014). At the same time, the employment rate was relatively high at 79.8% in 2013 (82.2% for men and 77.2% for women). This was more than 10 percentage points above the European average of 68.6%, where difference between men and women are larger (75% for men and 62.3% for women). The government projects the employment rate to rise to 81.6% by 2018 (Prime Minister's Office, 2014).

Figure 1.1. **Unemployment rate as % civilian labour force, Sweden, 2000-12**

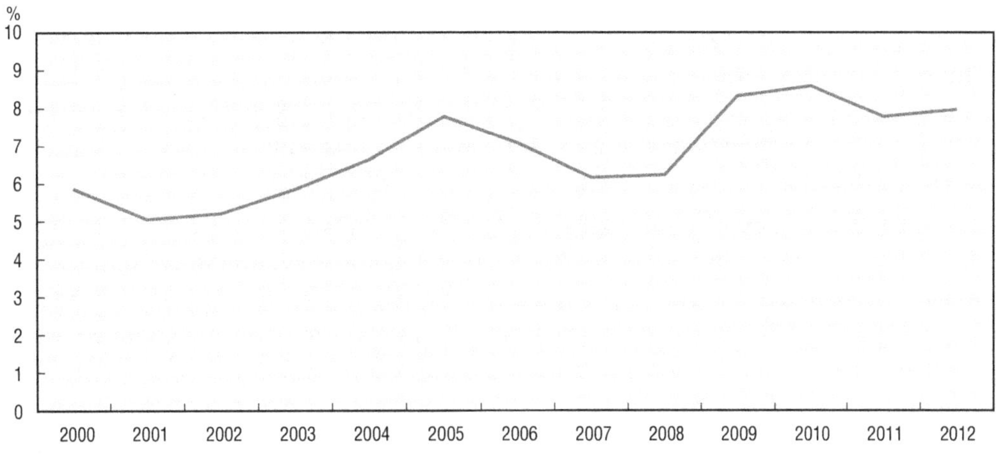

Source: OECD (2014), "Labour Force Statistics: Population and labour force", *OECD Employment and Labour Market Statistics* (database), *http://dx.doi.org/10.1787/data-00288-en.*

Figure 1.2. **Youth unemployment rate, Sweden, 2003-12**

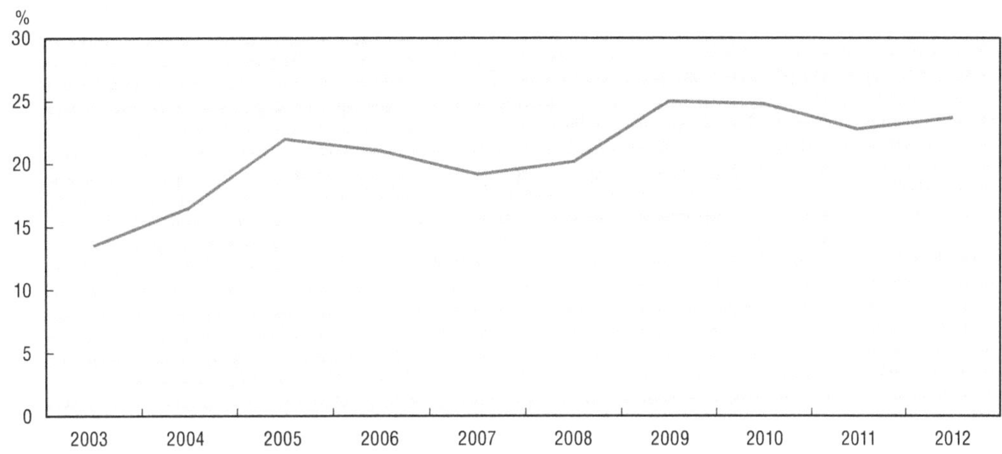

Source: OECD (2014), "Labour Force Statistics: Population and labour force", *OECD Employment and Labour Market Statistics* (database), *http://dx.doi.org/10.1787/data-00288-en.*

Employment and skills trends

The situation in Sweden is similar to many other OECD countries. There is a relatively high level of unemployment, however many employers are looking for skilled labour and are unable to fill job vacancies. Furthermore, unemployment levels vary across regions where the large metropolitan areas have strong growth and the smaller industrial towns have been hard hit by structural changes in the global economy. Recent studies indicate that the matching of skills in the labour market is problematic (Karlson and Skånberg, 2012). The challenge for policy is to attract new firms and jobs to an area, support firms and employees to proactively upgrade their skills, while also supporting the unemployed to find new jobs. However, Sweden has a strong skills foundation on which to build future competitiveness.

With regard to migrants, Sweden accepts a large number of refugees, which is among the largest in Europe. The large inflow to the country puts pressure, at least in short term, on the labour force and unemployment levels generally as it takes a longer time for refugees to enter employment compared to higher skilled immigrants.

The National Reform Programme provides an overview of the educational level of the workforce. In 2012, 47.9% of 30-34 year-olds had at least two years of tertiary education (53.7% for women and 42.4% for men) compared to the European level of 34.6%. This includes university education, advanced vocational training and higher vocational training. The drop-out rate from upper secondary school, measured as the proportion of the 18-24 year-old population who have not completed this education was 7.5% (6.3% for women and 8.5% for men) compared to an EU average of 13.5%.

The OECD's Survey of Adult Skills shows that young adults (aged 16-24) in Sweden have higher proficiency in literacy and problem solving and slightly lower proficiency in numeracy compared to the overall population. Some 16.1% of adults in Sweden (aged 16-65) attain the two highest levels of proficiency in literacy (Level 4 or 5) compared with an average of 11.8% of adults across all participating countries. Some 18.6% of adults in Sweden attain Level 4 or 5 in numeracy compared with an average of 12.4% of adults across all participating countries. Some 8.8% of adults are proficient at Level 3, the highest proficiency level, in problem solving in technology-rich environments (compared to an average of 5.8% of adults in all participating countries), while 35.2% attain proficiency Level 2 in problem solving (compared with an average of 28.2%).

A relatively large proportion of the adult population in Sweden have poor literacy, numeracy and problem-solving skills. Some 13.3% of adults attain only Level 1 or below in literacy proficiency (compared with the average of 15.5%) and 14.7% attain Level 1 or below in numeracy (compared with the average of 19.0%). Some 6.4% of Swedish adults (compared with 14.2% of adults in all participating countries) indicated that they had no prior experience with computers or lacked very basic computer skills, while 43.9% score at or below Level 1 in problem solving in technology-rich environments. This is slightly above the average, and similar to the levels found in Canada, Germany, the Netherlands and Norway.

Institutional framework for employment, skills, and economic development

Providing support for the unemployed is shared between the national and local levels of government in Sweden. Employment policy is mainly funded and provided through a national government agency, *Arbetsförmedlingen* (Af), while local governments take large responsibility in areas like social welfare and local economic development by providing support for unemployed individuals who are not qualified for unemployment benefits. Education and training is funded and provided by all levels of government. Economic development policies are also introduced by all levels of government but they are primarily co-ordinated at the regional level.

Figure 1.3 provides an overview of the most important ministries, organisations and actors with regard to employment, skills, and economic development policies divided by levels of government (European, national, regional and local).

The management of employment policies

Sweden is known for its long tradition of active labour market policy, where the unemployed are offered relatively generous benefits and training opportunities. This is combined in Sweden with employment regulation and a strong role for the social partners. In other words, Sweden has the "security" element of Danish "flexicurity", but not as much "flexibility", from the employers' perspective. While this is regulated by law, most other issues related to employment conditions are decided by the social partners through collective bargaining.

Figure 1.3. **Summary of institutional actors and programmes for employment, skills, and economic development**

Sweden: Institutional Map at National, Regional, and Local Levels

	Employment policy	Vocational education	Regional/economic development
European	European Social Fund (ESF)	Europass	European Regional Development Fund
National	Ministry of Labour	Ministry of Education	Ministry of Enterprise
	Arbetsförmedlingen	Universities	
	Försäkringskassan	University Colleges	*Tillväxtverket*
	Trygghetsrådet	*Yrkeshögskolan*	*Vinnova*
	IFAU	*Universitetskanslersämbetet*	*Tillväxtanalys*
Regional	Skills Platforms		
		Regional governments	
		Folkhögskola	*Länsstyrelsen*
		Kommunförbund	*Mälardalsrådet*
			Stockholm Business Alliance
Local	Local Government		
	Jobbtorg	Secondary schools	*Ung Företagsamhet*
		Komvux	
		SFI	
		Industry associations	

A key feature of Swedish employment policy is that it has an explicitly national perspective on the labour market. It emphasizes mobility over retraining for the local labour market, meaning that labour market policy operates with a national perspective on the matching of the supply and demand of skills. Retraining for local needs will only be given for skills where there is a local shortage. In turn, this means that there is in principle a tension with policies for local and regional development which aim at developing a specific region. This tension works out differently across the country depending on local opportunities and traditions of collaboration.

Historically, the emphasis on mobility was a key part of the Swedish model, where the social partners agreed on a macroeconomic framework for driving structural change. The unions and the employers agreed that the level of pay should be the same across the country, rather than determined through local settlements. The effect was that competitive firms were supported through lower salaries than they would otherwise pay, while uncompetitive firms were forced to change or close down since the salaries were higher than if they had been agreed locally. The outcome was a strong drive for structural change, where mobility and support for retraining of the unemployed created political support for what was otherwise dramatic change. This model lives on, for example in the unions' policy to "support the members' skills, not their particular jobs".

There is a tension with economic development policy, where local and regional governments have tended to emphasize the need to develop local resources. Local government have shown an interest in the management of labour market programmes with an interest in integrating them with social welfare policies.

Employment policies and their delivery have undergone substantial change over the past two decades. There is now a stronger emphasis on incentives for the unemployed, with more restrictions on the level of time a person can receive unemployment benefits, in combination with tax reductions to make work economically more rewarding to lower entrance thresholds into the labour market and improved job matching. The government has signalled the urgent need to improve outcomes for youth, the long-term unemployed, as well as immigrants (Prime Minister's Office, 2013).

Arbetsförmedlingen (Af) is responsible for the management and delivery of labour market polices in Sweden. The organisation has become more integrated over the last couple of years while certain services have been outsourced and/or opened for competition. The formerly semi-independent regional boards have been abolished to create a unified agency with streamlined work processes across the country. This has been combined with the strong use of performance objectives. Employment policy consists of about a dozen specific programmes which are regulated by the Parliament. In addition, the employment service implements programmes funded under immigration policies, including responsibility for the co-ordination of activities for newly arrived immigrants (Ministry of Finance, 2013b). Other agencies and local governments provide various programmes and services for this group.

The funding cycle begins with an elaborated budget presented to the Parliament by the government. The outcomes of the policies in the previous year are scrutinized in detail and serve as the foundation for the proposed budget. The Parliament decides on the strategic objectives as well as the overall level of funding for three broad categories of programmes, administration and individual benefits. Specific funding allocated to each category is decided by the government. The definition of objectives decided by the Parliament is expected to be broken down and applied by the employment service.

For 2014, the main objective of employment policies is to contribute to a well-functioning labour market (Ministry of Finance, 2013a). The objectives state that the matching of demand and supply is the main focus and that the priority is targeting people far removed from the labour market. The use of performance indicators by *Arbetsförmedlingen* means that these objectives are broken down and applied at all levels of service delivery. Collaboration with other agencies and policy areas is only allowed to the extent that it is compatible within this regulatory framework.

The government gives yearly instructions based on the budget-decision by Parliament. For *Arbetsförmedlingen*, in 2014 it is summarized in 16 major objectives and a number of restrictions and reporting requirements (Ministry of Labour, 2013). The first objectives are to break and prevent long-term unemployment. Other objectives include making stronger job-search requirements on unemployed individuals as well as strengthening the relationship between the employment service and employers. *Arbetsförmedlingen* reports yearly in similar categories. The reporting in 2013 (on activities in 2012) describes outcomes, activities and new methods and processes implemented during the year with the ambition to better fulfil the goals set by the government (*Arbetsförmedlingen*, 2013). Work processes have been further standardised and include a uniform registration process and a requirement to design an individual action plan within five days for an unemployed person. The risk of long-term unemployment should be assessed and lead to a set of early actions. *Arbetsförmedlingen* has not been assigned any primary responsibility for local or regional growth.

The total number of people registered with *Arbetsförmedlingen* in 2012 was 1.075 million (resulting in 20 million contacts), of which slightly more than half (549 000) went on to employment. Almost half of these people (252 000) were unemployed before while the other half were in labour market programmes (108 000) or had a job (176 000). Around half of the group which went on to employment is classified as being far from the labour market.

Several initiatives have been taken to target the long-term unemployed. One is the Job and Development Guarantee, which is now the flagship programme run by the employment service. It is divided into three phases, depending on how long an individual has been unemployed. Each phase has a set of standardized services to be offered. It includes the opportunity for a three month introduction to education and training in secondary schools with a non-traditional approach (Folkhögskola). Another instrument is a subsidy for hiring the unemployed called new-start jobs (115 000 in 2012).

General activities to promote skills development are discussed in terms of contributing to increased employment. 93 000 people received training in 2012 and 101 000 received work-placed training ("praktik"). A further 99 000 people received preparatory training designed for the long-term unemployed. There are also subsidies for commuting and relocation with the ambition that this improves the matching of the supply and demand of skills.

Other organisations involved in employment and related services

In addition to *Arbetsförmedlingen*, there are employment services set up by the social partners (e.g. employers and unions) called *Trygghetsrådet*, which assist people who are facing lay-off or employment termination. Typically, the organisation works with higher skilled individuals who require less intensive services than those who would engage with services under *Arbetsförmedlingen*. Almost 800 public and private organisations operate as complementary service providers. The outsourced services include job coaching and activities for at-risk groups.

There are overlapping clients with the agency for social security benefits, *Försäkringskassan* (FK), as well as with the local governments when it comes to people on welfare. One government strategy has been to separate these categories more clearly and also to formalize collaboration in the area of rehabilitation related to the labour market. There is much informal collaboration with local governments and social partners to identify common needs and to divide up roles and responsibilities. The local governments run a number of programmes for the unemployed who are not covered by the employment services, for example through *Jobbtorget*. There is a lot of work at the local level to reach people who have a weak position in the labour market, often through collaboration among a number of organisations.

Vocational education and training policies

The national government funds major programmes for skills development through its employment policy, social insurance policy and education policy. Employment policy and social insurance policy refer mainly to the training programmes offered through *Arbetsförmedlingen* and *Försäkringskassan*, often outsourced to others, such as the state-owned company Lernia. Under some circumstances, the agencies can allow individuals to take courses at universities while living on their respective benefits (rather than taking a student loan).

Education policy actors include the universities, higher vocational education (*Yrkeshögskolan*) organisations and non-traditional forms of education (*Folkbildning*). The definition of vocational education and training (VET) used by the government includes professional bachelors' degrees at the universities, in fields such as nursing and the training of teachers (Kuczera 2013:11). A definition of life-long learning includes university programmes which are offered mainly for adults, defined as over 25 and/or studying part-time (Statskontoret 2003). This includes courses given as distance education or "extensions" (evenings, weekends), while the first definition includes courses which have a vocational profile, for health professions, design professions, airline pilots and others. The universities have large autonomy to offer programmes with a unique profile, targeted at new sectors of the labour market within the framework regulation of degrees.

There are many sectors of training for adults. These programmes serve different purposes but overlap in terms of the clients they serve and/or service provision. The overlaps were particularly notable a decade ago, when there was a major increase in skills development programmes to meet the crisis of the late 1990s (Statskontoret 2003). Regular courses are provided for free and with subsidised loans. Courses can also be sold to companies and individuals, mainly as add-ons for practicing professionals.

Higher vocational education (*Yrkeshögskolan*) is a vocational post-secondary education pathway with some similarities to so-called polytechnics. They are run in short cycles, on a project basis. Funding decisions are made nationally based on a calculation of labour market need while the programmess are delivered by many types of education providers often integrated with other public systems (see Box 1.1).

An example of a service provider is Nackademin in the Stockholm area which provides a large number of vocational programmes. Around a third of the training with these programmes takes places in the workplace. This component is a key to assure relevance but also makes it similar in some ways to continental European apprenticeship systems (though under a different name). The reintroduction of an apprenticeship system was controversial in Sweden for a long time. Now there is a formal apprenticeship system (see below).

Thirdly, the national government funds certain secondary education courses which do not fit the traditional boundaries of secondary education (referred to as complementary education). These are often specialised vocational programmes. The government also funds un-traditional forms of education under *folkbildning*. These are evening courses (*studieförbund*) and boarding schools (*folkhögskolor*) with non-traditional methods originally set up to provide general education for adults organised in unions. Some of the boarding schools are funded through a programme for youth by *Arbetsförmedlingen*.

Local and regional governments fund secondary education, which includes various forms of secondary education for adults, especially *Komvux (kommunal vuxenutbildning)* and *Yrkesvux* (vocational training within *Komvux*), but also the non-traditional *folkhögskolor* and

Box 1.1. **Higher Vocational Education Programmes in Sweden**

Higher Vocational Education (*Yrkeshögskolan*) is a post-secondary form of education that combines theoretical and practical studies in close co-operation with employers and industry. Programmes are offered in specific fields where there is an explicit demand for competence. These programmes combine theory and practice and workplace training forms an integral part of their delivery. There are hundreds of programmes available across Sweden.

The largest number of programmes offered are in the fields of Business Finance and Administration, along with Sales and Manufacturing Technology. Other prominent areas include IT, Hospitality and Tourism, Health Care and Agriculture. Tuition is free of charge and many students are eligible for financial aid from the Swedish National Board for Student Aid (CSN). In order to safeguard the flexibility of the system, programmes can only be given twice and are then automatically terminated.

After graduating from an HVE programme, students are qualified to go straight into employment. Standards are set high in HVE programmes. Students are highly goal-oriented, looking to further themselves professionally.

Higher Vocational Education is delivered in co-operation between education providers and those employers and industries affected by the programme. All programmes therefore have a strong emphasis on workplace training. Employers and industry representatives play a significant role in the planning of an HVE programme and influence its content. Employers and industry contribute to programme content by taking part as lecturers, joining in projects, welcoming study visits and by offering work placements.

Source: Higher Vocational Education – Yrkeshögskolan in Sweden, programme description available at *www.yrkeshogskolan.se/Higher-Vocational-Education-HVE/*.

studieförbund. *Komvux* is a major provider of skills development and training for adults who want to upgrade or move into a new type of job. Some local governments have restricted access to those who have not completed regular secondary education.

Some of the courses funded by the employment service are similar, which led to discussions about possible co-ordination and collaboration (Statskontoret 2003). There have been various initiatives to support collaboration and integration of services. At the turn of the millennium many local governments introduced "Infotek" as a joint counselling service and "*Lärcentrum*", as a joint place of delivery. In 2010, the government introduced Skills platforms and asked local and regional actors of all kinds, including national agencies like the employment service, to participate in this effort to stimulate collaboration, co-ordinated by the regions (Prime Minister's Office 2013:27). Skills platforms are a revised form of the council "*Arbetsmarknadsråd*" which still exists in many counties.

The government aims to increase the level of education among youth as well as the use of the acquired skills. One instrument to reach younger dropouts is to invest in guidance counselling. Another instrument is the introduction of so-called work introduction measures. There is further support to develop the quality of workplace-learning and efforts by the national government to support local governments in their responsibility for young people up to the age of 20. The government also aims to improve the quality of higher education, especially the programmes for professional degrees such as engineering and nursing.

Apprenticeships

Apprenticeships were introduced as an experiment in 2008 and made permanent in 2011. Before that, the Swedish tradition was that vocational education should be an integrated part of secondary education. It is still part of the vocational secondary education system and described as a regular programme, but with an alternative way of teaching. This means that the degrees awarded are the same, rather than a unique set of degrees or occupations for the apprentices. More than half of the three year-programme is provided as work-based learning, while regular vocational programmes have 15 weeks of work-based learning.

Enrolment is less than 3 000 students per year. More than half of the students drop out, often to transfer into a regular vocational programmes. Studies indicate that this has to do with the weak background of the students who choose apprenticeships (Skolinspektionen, 2013). The programme is designed by the national government with subsidies for schools and local governments as well as for employers. There are partnerships with industry organisations for construction, transport, retail, health care and others.

Economic development policies

Economic development is a shared responsibility for all levels of government. Sweden has a long tradition of autonomy for the local and regional governments, like the other Nordic countries. Sweden even turns out as being more "federalist" than Australia, when measured in terms of the percentage of taxes which is raised by sub-national governments and the percentage of expenditure which is decided by sub-national governments. This means that in many areas broad policy goals are set by the Parliament and the national government, while the implementation is carried out by other levels of government or private providers. The two major exceptions are *Arbetsförmedlingen* and the agency for social insurance *(Försäkringskassan)*, which operate under the national government.

The local governments have a comprehensive responsibility for the planning and development of their area and for delivering services such as schools and welfare. Regional governments provide health care, public transport and some other services, including some forms of education. The national government operates agencies related to the national system of transfer payments (pensions, as well as benefits for the unemployed and sick), tertiary education and infrastructure agencies.

The leadership role for regional economic development is held by the elected regional (county) government *(Landsting)* in most of the regions, either directly or through an organisation which can be described as a Regional Development Agency, set up jointly with the local governments *(Regionförbund)*. There have been experiments with several models of RDAs and the original model is now only maintained in Stockholm and a few other regions. There, a national agency, a "prefecture" in the French tradition *(Länsstyrelsen)*, holds the leadership role and acts as a Regional Development Agency reporting to the Ministry of Finance.

All national agencies are expected to co-ordinate their regional and local activities with each other and with the local and regional governments under a joint regional planning framework known under various acronyms; RUP, RUS and (in Stockholm) RUFS. These are broad frameworks but contain specific workplans, where agencies and others agree on joint ambitions and priorities, within their respective regulatory frameworks.

They are often based on a careful analysis of regional and local challenges. The main data sources are the statistics produced by the employment service and Statistics Sweden (SCB) for the Regional Development Agencies.

Most agencies, including the employment service, operate with a smaller number of regions, covering a larger geography, which sometimes makes co-ordination difficult. *Arbetsförmedlingen* works with ten regions, covering geographies of various sizes, and an eleventh, functional region for specialised services. There is a general debate about merging the 21 counties into 6-8 lager regions to improve collaboration across the public sector (Ansvarskommittén, 2007).

One of the benefits of collaboration is that there can be a joint perspective on how to invest resources on issues where responsibilities are divided among several agencies, like skills development and fighting exclusion. In areas of the country where there is economic growth and expansion, new infrastructure and housing can be co-ordinated with projected business expansion plans. Education and training as well as services such as child care can also be aligned to these projections, or to upcoming needs for reskilling and transformation, in areas of the country where people become unemployed. Three core areas of regional collaboration are skills development, support for business and transport.

Since 1995, the European structural funds provide additional resources for regional development activities. The European Social Fund (ESF) supports skills development for the employed as well as the unemployed. ESF often supports projects together with *Arbetsförmedlingen*, *Försäkringskassan* and local governments. The European Regional Development Fund (ERDF) primarily supports infrastructure and projects in applied R&D. It is organised in eight regions (NUTS2), most of which cover several Swedish counties (NUTS3). Their design is currently in flux due to the new programming period. Programmes and strategies have been developed during 2013, which take an integrated view on the challenges facing these mega-regions and possible actions.

Intentions and outcomes

In an international perspective Sweden can be described as pursuing a policy of disciplined collaboration, rather than a geographical integration of all policy instruments. There is an encouragement of collaboration, but the division of responsibilities represents a major challenge. Employment policies have become more centralised over time but local governments play a big role as funders and service providers for the unemployed. Skills development is done by all levels of government. Co-ordination in general mainly takes place around the regional planning frameworks. This reflects Sweden's heritage of being a decentralised and uniform welfare state, with its inbuilt tensions.

However, there is a legacy of collaboration and local influence on policies. Over the last decade, the government has emphasized the separation of roles and responsibilities of the various agencies and sub-national governments related to job creation and economic development. This came after a decade when the government emphasized collaboration as a means to support economic development and skills development.

References

Ansvarskommittén (2007), Hållbar samhällsorganisation med utvecklingskraft. Slutbetänkande av Ansvarskommittén (*Sustainable community development organization; Final reports*) (SOU 2007:10), *www.regeringen.se/content/1/c6/07/75/20/a50fe36e.pdf*.

Arbetsförmedlingen (2013), *Arbetsförmedlingens* årsredovisning 2012 (*Employment Service Annual Report 2012*), Stockholm, *www.arbetsformedlingen.se/download/18.3485b9a713b6ad32ce18fb3/1401114605520/%C3%85resredovisning+2012.pdf.*

Jamet, S., T. Chalaux and V. Koen (2013), "Labour Market and Social Policies to Foster More Inclusive Growth in Sweden", *OECD Economics Department Working Papers*, No. 1023, OECD Publishing, Paris, *http://dx.doi.org/10.1787/5k4c0vtwpttj-en.*

Karlson, N. and O. Skånberg (2012), Matchning på den svenska arbetsmarknaden, Underlagsrapport 9 till Framtidskommissionen (*Job Matching in the Swedish Labour Market, Background Report 9 to the Futures Commission*), Stockholm: Statsrådsberedningen.

Ministry of Finance (2013a), Proposition 2013/14:1, Utgiftsområde (*expenditure*) 13, *www.regeringen.se/content/1/c6/22/37/09/a1839207.pdf.*

Ministry of Finance (2013b), Proposition 2013/14:1, Utgiftsområde (*expenditure*) 14, *www.regeringen.se/content/1/c6/22/37/09/e0708c49.pdf.*

Ministry of Labour (2013), Regleringsbrev för budgetåret 2014 avseende *Arbetsförmedlingen (Appropriations for the fiscal year 2014 regarding Employment Service).*

OECD (2013), *OECD Survey of Adult Skills – Sweden Country Note*, OECD, Paris, *www.oecd.org/site/piaac/Country%20note%20-%20Sweden.pdf.*

OECD (2010), *OECD Territorial Reviews: Sweden 2010*, OECD Publishing, *http://dx.doi.org/10.1787/9789264081888-en.*

Kuczera, M. (2013), "A skills beyond school commentary on Sweden", *OECD Reviews on Vocational Education and Training*, OECD Publishing, Paris, *www.oecd.org/edu/skills-beyond-school/ASkillsBeyondSchoolCommentaryOnSweden.pdf.*

Prime Minister's Office (2014), *Sweden's National Reform Programme 2014*, Europe 2020 – the EU's strategy for smart, sustainable and inclusive growth.

Prime Minister's Office (2013), *Sweden's National Reform Programme 2013*, Europe 2020 – the EU's strategy for smart, sustainable and inclusive growth.

Skolinspektionen (2013), *En kvalitetsgranskning av gymnasial lärlingsutbildning (A quality of secondary apprenticeship)*, Rapport 2013:02, *www.skolinspektionen.se/Documents/Kvalitetsgranskning/larling-gy/kvalgr-larling-gy-slutrapport.pdf.*

Statistics Sweden (2013), *Ungdomsarbetslöshet – jämförbarhet i statistiken mellan ett antal europeiska länder (Youth Unemployment – comparability of statistics from a number of European countries)*, Arbetsmarknads- och utbildningsstatistik 2013:1, *www.scb.se/statistik/_publikationer/AM0401_2013A01_BR_AM76BR1301.pdf.*

Statskontoret (2003), Kommunernas ansvar för vuxnas lärande – Vad bör staten göra? *(Municipal responsibility for adult learning – What should the state do?)*, Rapport nr 2003:10, Stockholm, *www.skolinspektionen.se/Documents/Kvalitetsgranskning/larlingvux/kvalgr-larlingvux-slutrapport.pdf*

Chapter 2

Overview of the Swedish case study areas

To better understand the role of the local level in contributing to job creation and productivity, the OECD Local Job Creation review examined local activities in two Swedish regions: 1) Gävle; and 2) Stockholm. This chapter provides a labour market and economic overview of each region as well as the results from an OECD LEED statistical tool which looks at the relationship between skills supply and demand at the sub-national level.

Overview of the regions

As part of this review of local job creation policies, in-depth fieldwork has been undertaken in two local case study areas (Stockholm and Gävle).

Stockholm

The city of Stockholm is the centre of a major metropolitan area with more than two million inhabitants, of which about 900 000 live in the city. The city of Stockholm is in many ways integrated in the planning and collaborative framework of the county of Stockholm. The region for Stockholm of *Arbetsförmedlingen* runs 11 offices in the city and serves a population of more than one million people.

Figure 2.1. **Map of Stockholm county and its surrounding regions**

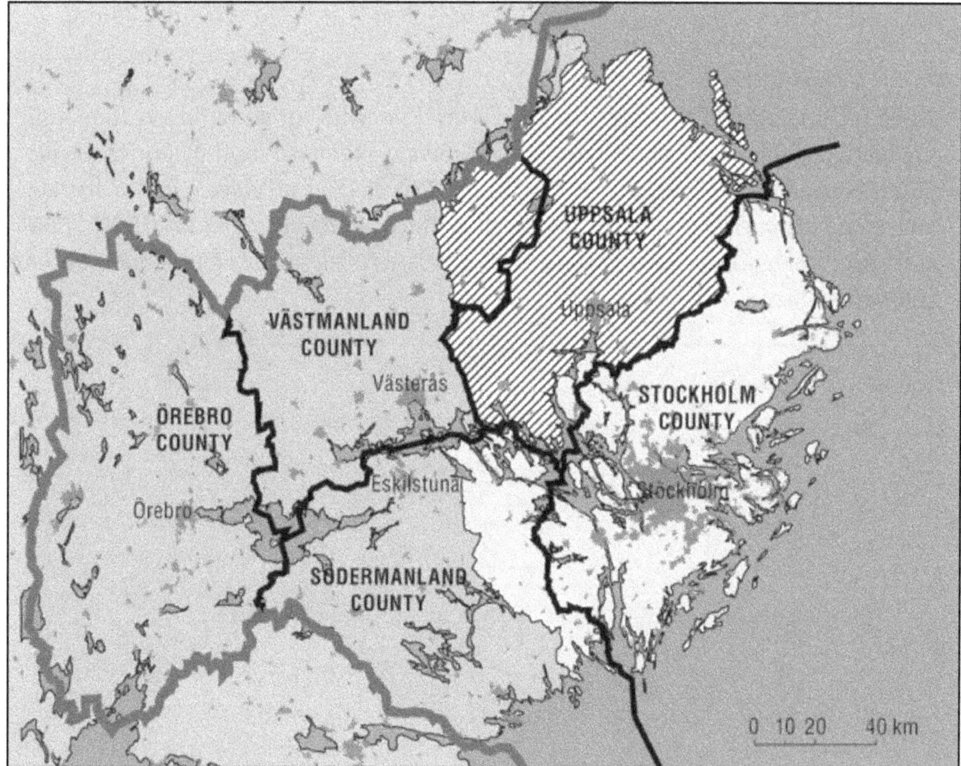

Source: OECD (2006), *OECD Territorial Reviews: Stockholm, Sweden 2006*, OECD Publishing, *http://dx.doi.org/10.1787/9789264022539-en.*

Like other capitals, Stockholm has a large proportion of major company headquarters and administrative centres. This means that there is a substantial labour market for highly skilled individuals and generally the demand is higher than the supply. The main large export-oriented industries are in Information and Communication Technologies (ICT) and pharmaceuticals, while other major industries are in construction, finance and retail. Stockholm has not been as hard hit as other parts of the country with a more one-sided base in heavy industry. There are at the same time many signs of overheating, such as congested traffic and a scarcity of housing.

Stockholm has a large number of higher education and vocational training institutions, as well as a dynamic sector of secondary education where public and private providers compete for students. There is also a large sector of fee-based education, paid for by individuals or employers.

The most recent planning document was developed for the European structural funds based on other regional planning documents. It points out that skills levels and employment rates are higher than in other European capitals, while in school achievement, the proportion of private companies and the level of integration (of the young and foreign born) is lower in Stockholm (Länsstyrelsen, 2013). Like in other metropolitan regions, there are pockets of areas with higher levels of immigrants and unemployment. There is furthermore a steady inflow of refugees from countries such as Syria and of relatives of other immigrants, which means an inflow of low-skilled labour, for which the demand is generally lower than the supply. These areas have been targeted by local as well as national policies to fight exclusion through skills development projects to bring at risk-groups closer to the labour market.

The city (local government) of Stockholm is a strong actor in the area. It funds all primary and secondary education for youth and a large part of secondary education for adults. It funds substantial programmes for individuals who are outside of the regular labour market and many activities for immigrants. It funds roads and other infrastructure projects and owns housing companies.

There is an informal council for collaboration in this wider area, known as the Lake Mälaren district (Mälardalsrådet), where more than a third of the population of Sweden live (e.g. 3.8 of 9.6 million individuals). The council is especially active in the joint planning of infrastructure, where all local governments have contributed funding out of their local taxes for the new railway tunnel under Stockholm, which will ease commuting and further integrate the labour markets of this region.

Regional economic planning is done by county, which means that the city of Stockholm is part of the planning framework for Stockholm county. The surrounding counties make their own plans, where Gävle is the centre of a county which stretches further north. Employment policy has a different geography, where the city of Stockholm forms its own region (Marknadsområde) with the suburb Lidingö and the island Gotland, while the county of Stockholm is divided into a northern and a southern region and integrated with the nearest counties.

The European regional development fund operates with a third version of regions (NUTS2). Here, the county of Stockholm is a region of its own, while all the surrounding counties (Uppsala, Västmanland, Örebro, Södermanland and Östergötland) form a banana-shaped region around – and much dependent on – Stockholm, known as East Midsweden. Gävle belongs to a set of three counties to its west rather than north (Gävleborg, Dalarna, Värmland) – a different region from the employment policy region, known as "North Midsweden".

Gävle

Gävle is in many ways different from Stockholm. The county consists of two sub-regions with very different identities. The southern part (Gästrikland) is dominated by Gävle and the industrial base, while the northern part (Hälsingland) consists of several small towns, where there is a high level of employment in agriculture. *Arbetsförmedlingen* runs a large office in Gävle, which is co-ordinated by the regional headquarters in Östersund.

It is a provincial capital and a regional centre with a university college and a few national agencies have located their headquarters in the city. However, the county has the lowest level of tertiary education among the Swedish counties. Many young people move to Uppsala or Stockholm for education and work. The level of employment among immigrants is one of the lowest in the country.

The surrounding area of Gävle has a strong industrial tradition in steel, pulp and paper as well as food (e.g. coffee and candy products). Sandvik is a global company, producing materials for car manufacturing and others, located west of Gävle in Sandviken. Pulp and paper is produced in many factories along the coast. Many of these industries have been hit by weakened demand and pressures to cut costs. As a secondary effect, the port of Gävle has laid off people.

The leadership role in regional planning and collaboration has been held since 2007 by a Regional Development Agency set up by the regional and local governments (*Regionförbundet Gävleborg*). It is merged with the regional government (*Landsting*) into Region Gävleborg, to take advantage of synergies, including the right of taxation and an elected assembly. The local government of Gävle is a strong actor in the regional as well as the local arena. Like the local government of Stockholm, it funds, among other things, education, infrastructure and programmes for people outside of the regular labour market.

Comparisons across the case study areas

Commuting Patterns

Commuting into Stockholm for employment is extensive from other big cities in Sweden, including Uppsala (200 000), Västerås (140 000), Södertälje (90 000) and Nyköping (50 000), and further cities within two hours by train, which include Norrköping (130 000), Linköping (150 000), Eskilstuna (100 000), Örebro (140 000) and Gävle (100 000). The inbound commuting to Stockholm from other counties in 2011 was almost 30 000 people from Uppsala county to the north, almost 16 000 from Södermanland to the south and almost 5 000 from Västmanland to the west. Interestingly, the commuting from the other metropolitan areas was substantial from the Gothenburg area (Västra Götaland) almost 10 000 and from Malmö (Skåne) almost 8 500. The outbound commuting to these other counties from Stockholm at the same time was more than 20 000 (Statistics Sweden, 2014).

Table 2.1. **Commuting patterns to Stockholm**

County	Commuting to Stockholm	Commuting from Stockholm
Uppsala	28 995	8 138
Södermanland	15 574	3 548
Västmanland	4 917	1 623
Västra Götaland	9 540	4 531

Source: Statistics Sweden, 2014.

The commuting from Gävle (Gävleborg) to Stockholm was almost 3 000, while commuting in the other direction was about 1 100. Inbound commuting to Gävle was largest from Uppsala county (almost 3 000), with a smaller number going to Uppsala (2 000). Outbound commuting to Västernorrland to the north was almost 1 000 while the inbound commuting was more than 500. Inbound commuting from Dalarna to the west was slightly more than 1 000 while outbound commuting was slightly less (Statistics Sweden 2014).

Table 2.2. **Commuting patterns to Galve**

County	Commuting to Gävle	Commuting from Gävle
Stockholm	1 122	2 923
Uppsala	2 936	1 969
Västernorrland	521	921

Source: Statistics Sweden, 2014.

Figure 2.2. **Commuting patterns to and from Swedish regions**

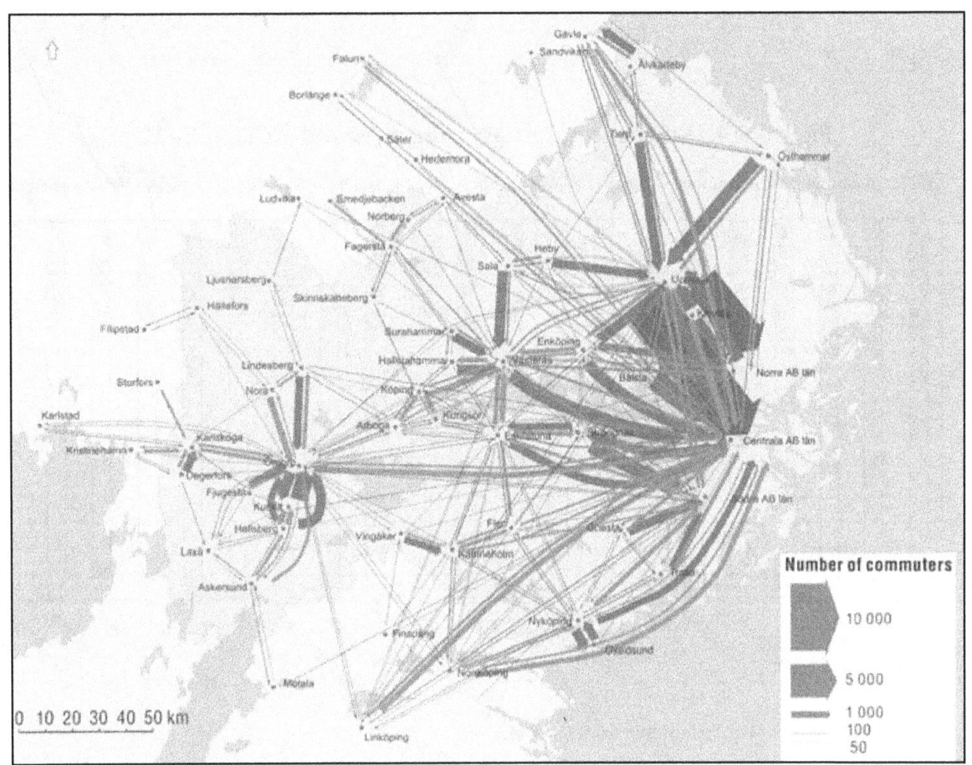

Source: OECD (2006), *OECD Territorial Reviews: Stockholm, Sweden 2006*, OECD Publishing, *http://dx.doi.org/10.1787/9789264022539-en.*

Unemployment dynamics

Figure 2.3 shows the unemployment rate by region across Sweden. In 2012, Gävleborg (which includes Gävle) has the highest unemployment rate in Sweden – almost 10%. Stockholm has one of the lower unemployment rates at just over 6%.

Educational attainment

Figure 2.4 shows education attainment at the regional level across Sweden. In 2012, Gävleborg has the lowest share of the population with a tertiary qualification. A large

Figure 2.3. **Unemployment rate, Sweden TL3 regions, 2012**

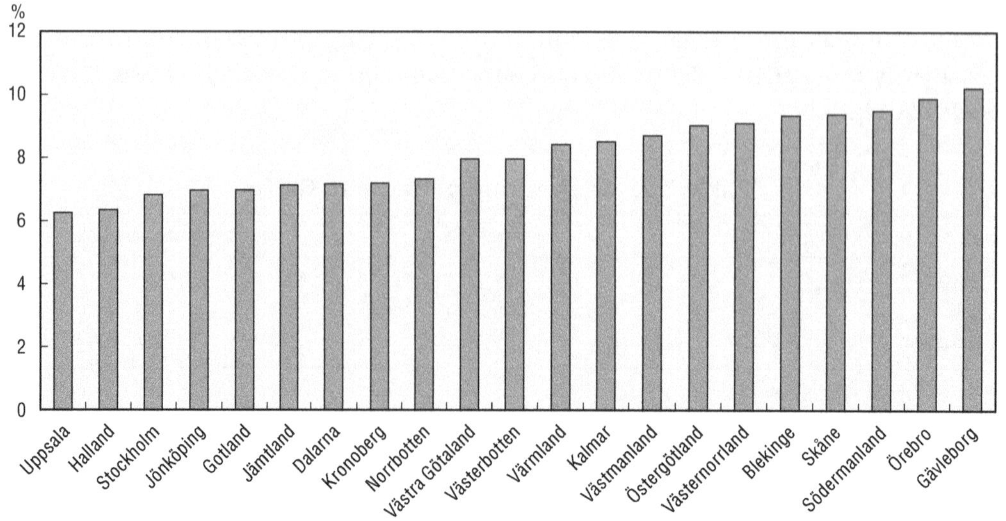

Source: OECD, 2012.

Figure 2.4. **Educational attainments, Sweden TL3, 2012**

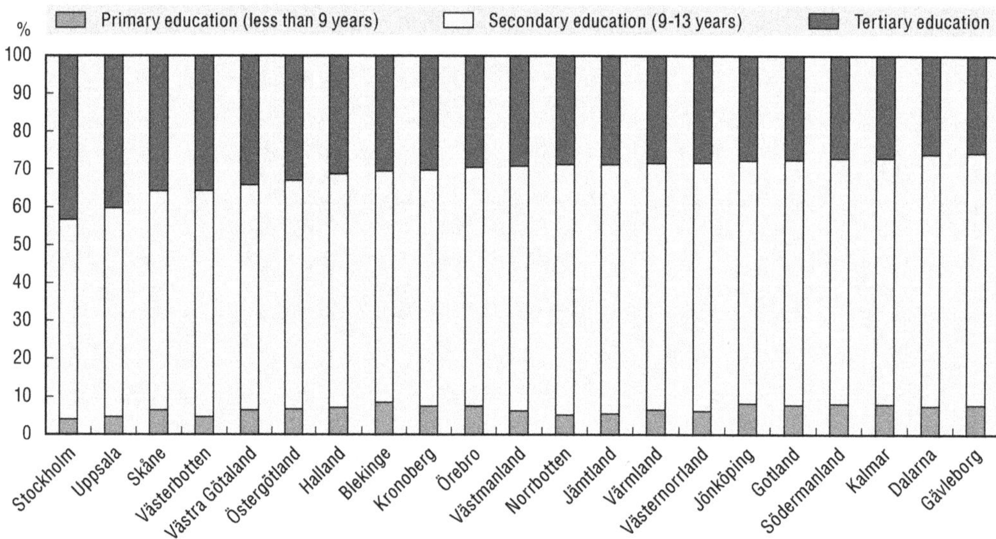

Source: Swedish Register of Education, Statistics Sweden.

proportion of individuals in this region have secondary education as their highest level of educational attainment. Stockholm has the highest.

Industry structure

Industry structure dictates the types of jobs in a region and the qualifications that workers must meet in finding employment. Figure 2.5 shows the industrial structure across TL3 regions in Sweden. Compared to Stockholm and to most other regions in Sweden, Gävle has a larger share of employment in the construction industry. Stockholm has the largest share of employment in financial and insurance related activities. The industrial structure of the metropolitan area clearly shows the benefits of its well-education population and the number of high quality jobs in the region.

Figure 2.5. **Share of employment by industry, Sweden TL3 regions, 2010**

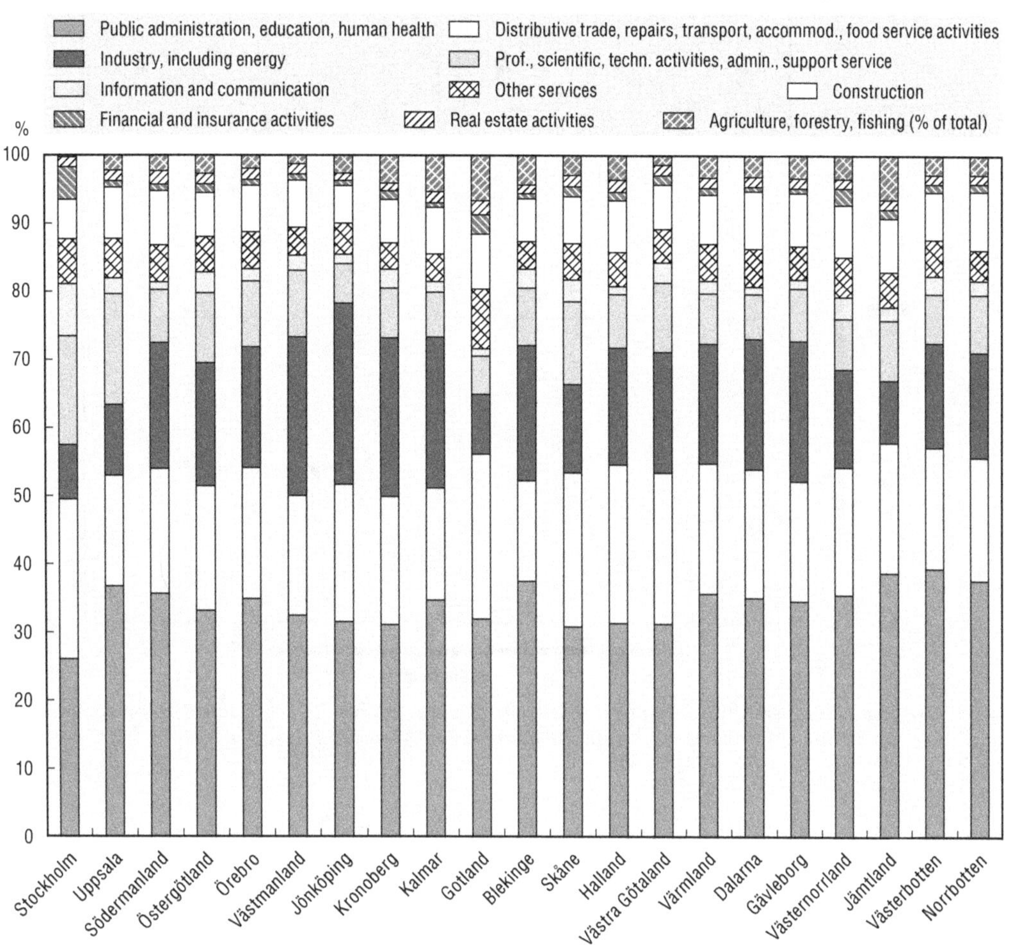

Source: OECD (2013), "Small regions, TL3: Regional labour market", *OECD Regional Statistics* (database), *http://dx.doi.org/10.1787/data-00528-en*.

Balance between skills supply and demand at the sub-national level

The LEED Programme has developed a statistical tool to understand the balance between skills supply and demand within local labour markets (Froy, Giguère and Meghnagi, 2012). In the Swedish context, this tool can help to provide policy makers with an understanding of skills mismatches, which may occur at the sub-national level. It can inform place-based policy approaches at the local level.

Looking at the figure above, in the top-left corner (skills gaps and shortages), demand for high skills is met by a supply of low skills, a situation that results in reported skills gaps and shortages. In the top-right corner, demand for high skills is met by an equal supply of high skills resulting in a high-skill equilibrium. This is the most desired destination of all high performing local economies. At the bottom-left corner the demand for low skills is met by a supply of low skills resulting in a low-skill equilibrium. The challenge facing policymakers is to get the economy moving in a north-easterly direction towards the top-right corner. Lastly, in the bottom-right corner, demand for low skills is met by a supply of high skills resulting in an economy where what high skills are available are not utilised. This leads to the out migration of talent, underemployment, skill under-utilisation, and attrition of human capital, all of which signal missed opportunities for creating prosperity.

Figure 2.6. **Understanding the relationship between skills supply and demand**

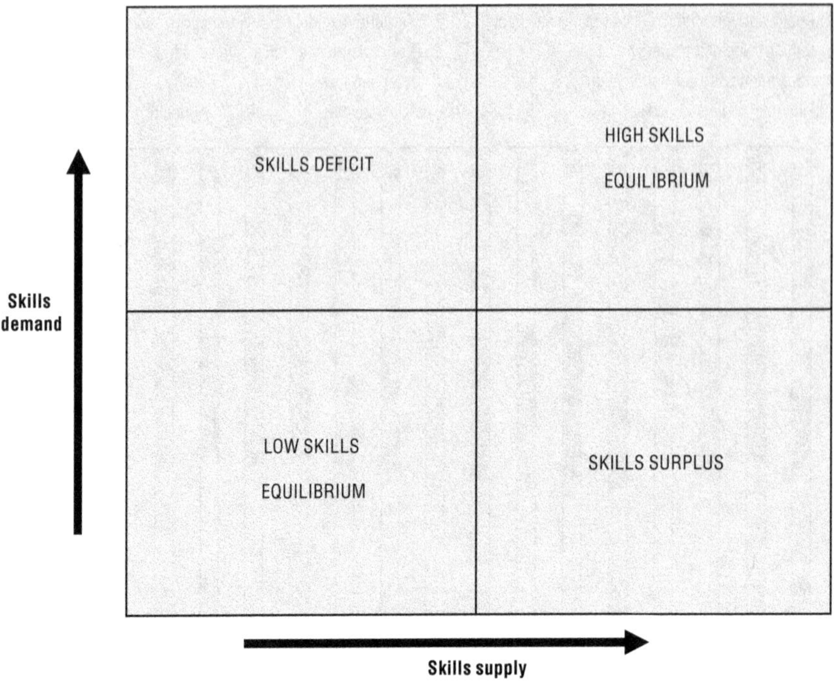

Source: Froy, F. and S. Giguère (2010), "Putting in Place Jobs that Last: A Guide to Rebuilding Quality Employment at Local Level", *OECD Local Economic and Employment Development (LEED) Working Papers*, No. 2010/13, OECD Publishing, Paris, *http://dx.doi.org/10.1787/5km7jf7qtk9p-en*.

Box 2.1. **Explaining the diagnostic tool**

The analysis is carried out at Territorial Level 3 regions (regions with populations ranging between 150 000-800 000). The supply of skills was measured by the percentage of the population with post-secondary education. The demand for skills was measured by the percentage of the population employed in medium-high skilled occupations. Regions are also classified in relation to the average state unemployment rate. The indices are standardised using the inter-decile method and are compared with the national median. Further explanations on the methodology can be found in Froy, Giguère and Meghnagi, 2012.

Source: Froy, F., S. Giguère and M. Meghnagi (2012), "Skills for Competitiveness: A Synthesis Report", *OECD Local Economic and Employment Development (LEED) Working Papers*, No. 2012/09, OECD Publishing, *http://dx.doi.org/10.1787/5k98xwskmvr6-en*.

This typology was applied to Sweden regions, including the case study regions of Gävle and Stockholm – see Figures 2.7 and 2.8 below.

The results from this analysis show variations across the regions. Stockholm falls into the high-skills equilibrium quadrant, clearly demonstrating the competitive advantage of the region relative to other areas of the country. Stockholm's relative position within a high-skills equilibrium does not change between 2001 and 2011. In 2011, Gävleborg (which is where Gävle is located) falls within the skills shortage or gaps quadrant, which shows that there is greater demand for skills than the supply. Between 2001-11, Gävleborg moved from a low-skills equilibrium (indicating a large number of poor quality jobs in the region) to the skills surpluses and gaps quadrant. Looking at this trend analysis, this would seem

Figure 2.7. **Balancing skills supply and demand in Sweden, 2001**

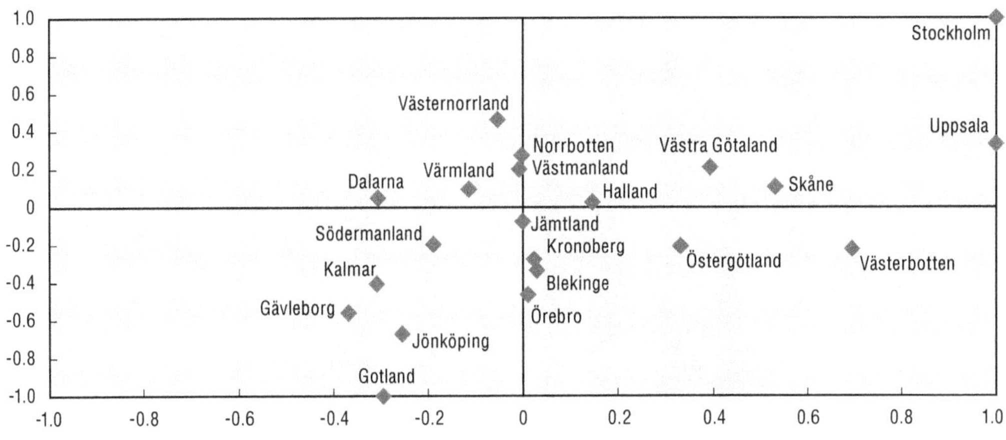

Figure 2.8. **Balancing skills supply and demand in Sweden, 2011**

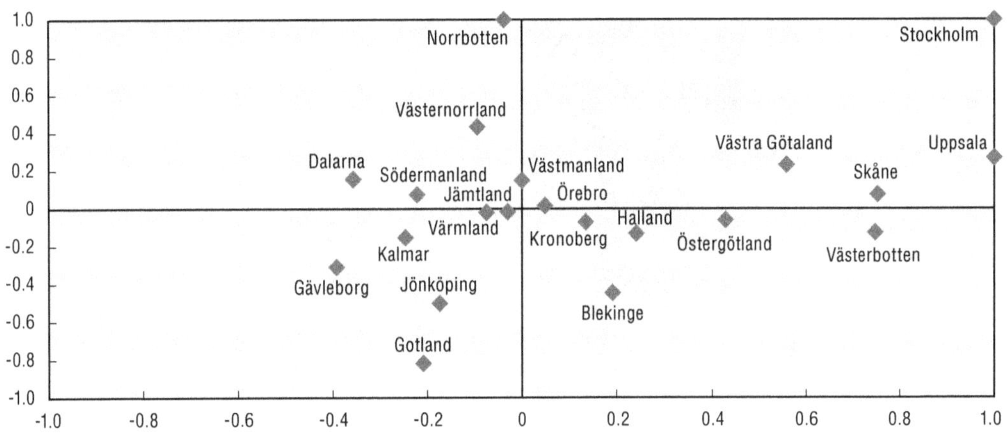

to indicate that low-skilled jobs have reduced and there are a number of employers in the region looking for higher skills than contained within the local population. The results comparing the supply and demand of skills can be displayed geographically to further articulate regional differences across Sweden (see Figure 2.9). This map clearly articulates differences between north and south of Sweden. Northern regions of Sweden fall into mismatches in the supply and demand of skills. The regions, which are in a high-skills equilibrium tend to be where there are strong educational institutions, which clearly have an impact on the quality of jobs in the local area.

Figure 2.9. **Skills supply and demand, 2011 – Geographical representation**

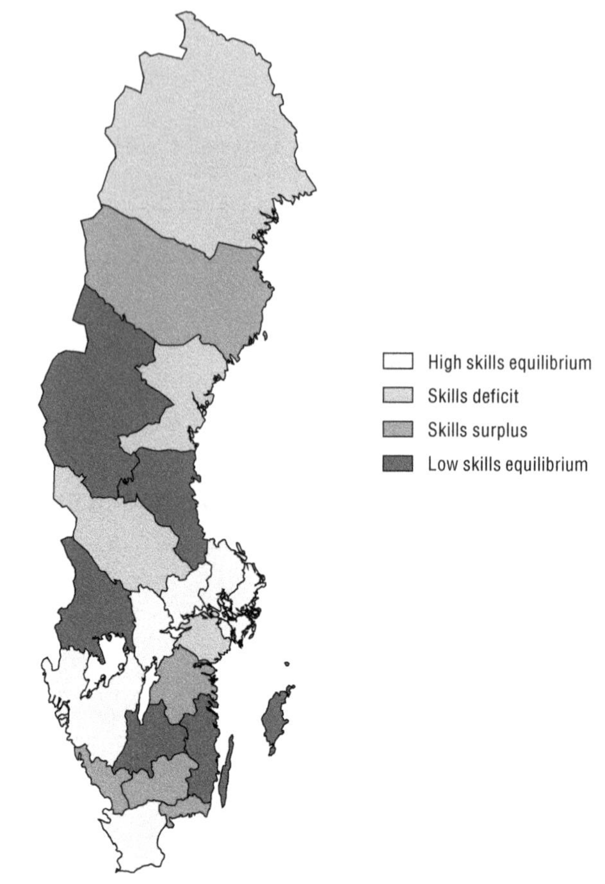

References

Froy, F. and S. Giguère (2010), "Putting in Place Jobs that Last: A Guide to Rebuilding Quality Employment at Local Level", *OECD Local Economic and Employment Development (LEED) Working Papers*, No. 2010/13, OECD Publishing, Paris, *http://dx.doi.org/ 10.1787/5km7jf7qtk9p-en.*

Froy, F., S. Giguère and M. Meghnagi (2012), "Skills for Competitiveness: A Synthesis Report", *OECD Local Economic and Employment Development (LEED) Working Papers*, No. 2012/09, OECD Publishing, Paris, *http://dx.doi.org/10.1787/5k98xwskmvr6-en.*

The County Administrative Board of Stockholm (2013): *Analysis of trends in the Stockholm region. The Structural Funds 2014-2020*, Stockholm, *www.lansstyrelsen.se/stockholm/SiteCollectionDocuments/Sv/publikationer/2013/R2013-10-Analys-strukturfonder.pdf.*

OECD (2006), "OECD Territorial Reviews: Stockholm, Sweden 2006", OECD Publishing, *http://dx.doi.org/ 10.1787/9789264022539-en.*

Statistics Sweden (2014), Fakta om län, Arbetsmarknad (*Facts about labour at the county level*).

Chapter 3

Local Job Creation Dashboard findings in Sweden

This chapter highlights findings from the Local Job Creation Dashboard in Sweden. The findings are discussed through the four thematic areas of the OECD review: 1) better aligning policies and programmes to local employment development; 2) adding value through skills; 3) targeting policy to local employment sectors and investing in quality jobs; and 4) being inclusive.

Results from the dashboard

This section of the report presents the main findings from the in-depth fieldwork undertaken in Sweden to look at the implementation of employment and skills policies. In the following section, each of the four priority areas of the OECD review are presented and discussed. The full results of the Local Job Creation Dashboard analysis for Sweden are presented in Figure 3.1 below.

Figure 3.1. **Overview of results from Local Job Creation Dashboard**

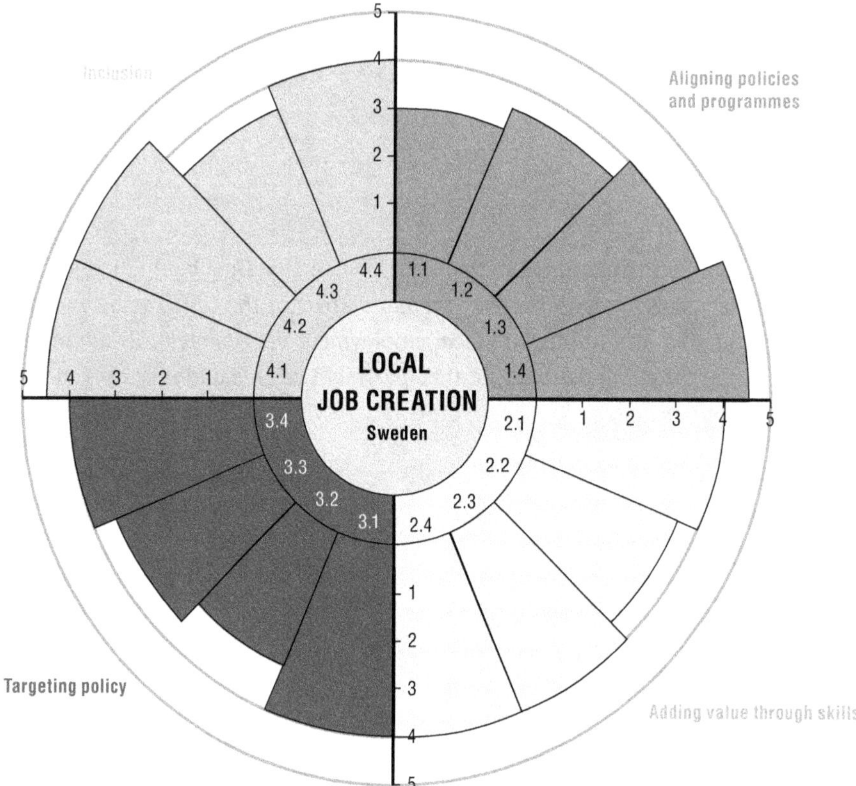

Theme 1: Better aligning policy and programmes to local economic development

Flexibility in the delivery of employment and vocational training policies

The OECD defines flexibility as "the possibility to adjust policy at its various design, implementation and delivery stages to make it better adapted to local contexts, actions carried out by other organisations, strategies being pursued, and challenges and opportunities faced" (Giguère and Froy, 2009). Flexibility deals with the latitude that exists in the management system of the employment system, rather than the flexibility in the

Figure 3.2. **Dashboard results: Better aligning programmes and policies to local economic development**

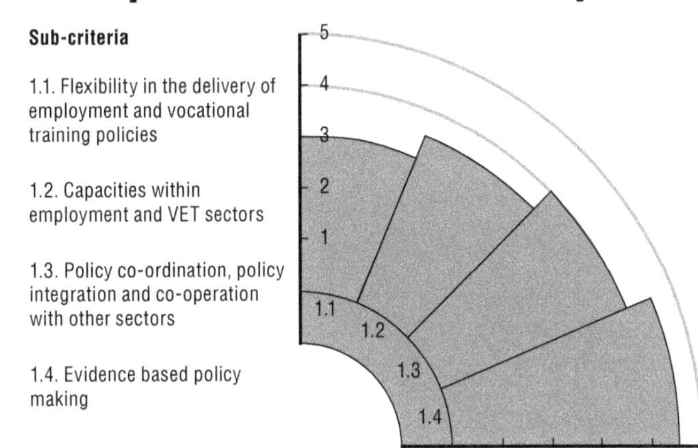

labour market itself. The achievement of local flexibility does not necessarily mean that governments need to politically decentralise (Giguère and Froy, 2009). Governments just need to give sufficient latitude when allocating responsibilities in the fields of designing policies and programmes; managing budgets; setting performance targets; deciding on eligibility; and outsourcing services.

Flexibility within the management of employment services

Flexibility is a difficult issue in Sweden, since employment policy is designed centrally to be carried out in a uniform fashion across the country. Compared to other OECD countries, flexibility in the management of employment policies is low. Employment policies take a national perspective on the labour market with an emphasis on mobility rather than re-training people to stay in a particular area. Retraining can be offered if there is an identified skills shortage. Employment programmes are designed nationally by the government and with heavy involvement by the Parliament in the specific details. The whole suite of about a dozen programmes has to be implemented locally. Work processes are streamlined to ensure that clients are treated in a uniform fashion across the country.

A positive side-effect is that the local offices of *Arbetsförmedlingen* can work with clients who live in any part of the country. At the same time, this emphasis on uniformity may make it more difficult to explain to clients why local differences in skills shortages lead to different treatment across the country (Rothstein, 1994).

In the area of budget management, budgets are set nationally with almost no possibility to move funds between allocated programme budget lines. Funding can be redistributed geographically within the regions (*Marknadsområde*) but not across the programmes without prior permission by the central level. During the OECD study visit, some stakeholders noted the inefficiencies returning un-spent funds which programmes can create, when there is a need for more funding for other programmes.

Limited local flexibility is reinforced by an elaborate list of performance targets which are set nationally (see Table 3.1). While local offices are consulted in this process, they are not rewarded for undertaking additional activities beyond the performance management framework, which could lead to innovation. The performance objectives include inputs and procedures (e.g. number of training courses given), take up rates (e.g. number of people completing training), client satisfaction (e.g. opinions of clients on the courses given) and

Table 3.1. **Performance Management Framework: Suggested national targets for 2014, compared to targets and achievements for 2013**

Perspective	Measurement	Proposed target 2014	Target 2013	Achievement 2013
Clients	To work	464 200	449 800	464 217
	Contacts with employers	480 215	480 215	470 538
	To work and training, early stage programme (JOB)	57 000	51 500	55 665
	To work and training, latest stage program	14 500		13 000
	To work and training, youth	48 700	48 650	50 146
	To work and training, new immigrants	18 700	16 891	18 713
	To work and training, disabled	55 000	50 479	52 899
	To work and training, introduction (etablering)	2 700		1 747
	Percentage of employers satisfied with AF's dealing with their issues	90%	90%	91.7%
	Percentage of employers who received enough applicants to fill their vacancies	85%	85%	82.3%
	To work or training within 90 days after an activity by AF	(Under investigation)		
Line of business	Market share of companies	0% unchanged	+6%	+6.3%
	Suggestions of applicants to employers	40%	40%	26.3%
	Workplace activities, JOB	60%	60%	44.3%
	Workplace activities, UGA	50%	50%	36.2%
	Workplace activities, etableringsuppdraget	50%	50 % proposed but not decided, statistics missing	40%
	Follow-up on suggested applicants to employers	90%	98%	78.4%
	Percentage matchable 30 days after an activity by AF	(Under investigation)		
Staff	Dialogues on development	At least average grade7	At least average grade 7	6.6
	Percentage on duty (i.e. not on sick-leave)	70%	70%	60.6%
Finance	Accumulated net result on government grant 1:1	+ 0.0% – 3.0%	+ 0.0% – 3.0%	-2.5%
	Accumulated net results on government grants 1:3, 1:4 and the commission on introduction (etablering)	+ 0.0% – 3.0%	+ 0.0% – 3.0%	1:3, 1:4 ca -1.5%, The commission on introduction (etablering) greatly under-utilized > 20%

the achievement of socio-economic outcomes (e.g. lowering of the unemployment rate). Over 75 % of the targets are outcomes-based. This system has evolved from an original set which was simpler but was generally thought to produce unwanted side-effects. The new performance targets are among the most developed within Swedish public management. The performance framework is related to the Balanced Scorecard which is used internally. It can be broken down at various levels and even by individual employees. This is in contrast to the previous model, where all managers were publicly graded in either red or green colours out of 10 points.

Accountability is almost entirely upwards in the hierarchy and to the government. The local employment agency reports to *Arbetsmarknadsrådet*, which is a regional council that provides guidance on aspects of the work of the agency. This information-sharing is in contrast to the older model before 2008, when *Arbetsförmedlingen* was a conglomerate of 21 semi-independent regional organisations by county – each of which had its own board while operating under a national board and a national regulatory framework.

Outsourcing of operations can be an instrument to strengthen flexibility, but it may also make it more difficult to adjust pre-set programmes to individual needs. There is a push by the government to outsource operations by *Arbetsförmedlingen* and to open up for competition to private companies in areas like recruitment and matching of demand and supply. The outsourcing is carried out nationally, based on an inventory of local needs. This refers to job coaching and skills development. The services are provided by outside contractors and so-called complementary actors are generally considered flexible enough to meet local and regional needs. The contractors are given strict targets in terms of the types of people helped and the types of services to be given and there is therefore limited flexibility, but also a sense of fair treatment. There is some room for flexibility for the employment service. For example, there is often no limit to the amount of courses which can be purchased under these contracts.

Overall, the local offices of *Arbetsförmedlingen* are able to provide services to most individuals who come to their offices. Services are targeted towards the unemployed and to those who are the furthest away from the labour market. People with a job can be treated as transfer applicants (*ombytessökande*), which is important for *Arbetsförmedlingen* in its relationship with local employers.

Vocational education and training

A large share of vocational education and training is provided by *Arbetsförmedlingen* through their contractors. Local stakeholders (e.g. employers) can request special training programmes to meet local needs but the approval process can be burdensome. Contracting takes a lot of time due to frequent legal action/obstruction. It is very common that the choice of contractor is challenged through the administrative courts. The service can be provided much quicker when there is already an outsourced programme in place.

Local governments provide similar types of training through *Komvux*, with less regulation, which means that it can be developed and delivered more efficiently. Programmes are generally run in-house by the secondary schools which are part of *Komvux*. Volumes and eligibility depend on local decisions. Additional programmes and courses are offered by the non-traditional boarding schools (*folkhögskola*), evening schools (*studieförbund*), universities and private companies. All of these are quite flexible but depend on funding as well as demand.

Further flexibility is provided by the system of charter schools, which makes it easy for the private sector to set up schools which receive public funding. An example in the Gävle area is the vocational secondary school – Göranssonska skolan – set up by Sandvik, an international company based in Sandviken. The school runs very attractive programmes in a way that is generally not possible through the public system. Other private initiatives with an impact on the system of vocational training are the trainee-programmes run by major corporations, such as Korsnäs in pulp and paper.

The nationally funded higher vocational education system (*Yrkeshögskolan*) provides higher vocational programmes which have some similarities with the courses provided by *Arbetsförmedlingen*. The contracts are for a limited time and awarded after a competitive process. This system is quite flexible by terminating old programmes and shifting the resources to new fields or new parts of the country. From a local perspective, this can be felt as a limit to flexibility, when popular programmes are terminated even while the local need may remain. The short programme cycles can reduce programme attractiveness to employers and prospective students.

Future vocational/adult training provision by nationally funded organisations is planned on the basis of national regulation and targets. It is also planned on the basis of an analysis of the local and national economic context. In general, secondary education is an area where local goverrnments have full autonomy. They often collaborate with each other within regions for secondary schools (*gymnasieregioner*) and the regional association (in some counties) for collaboration among local governments (*kommunförbund*).

Capacities within employment and VET sectors

When it comes to employment services, financial resources are perceived to be fully sufficient for delivering objectives. At the same time, during the OECD study visit, local stakeholders noted that they see resources as limited for innovative initiatives. Furthermore, they argue that there is a shortage for some programmes within the employments service while other programmes show a surplus at the end of the year. More flexibility with programme budgets would enable local stakeholders to shift resources to programmes in demand at the local level.

Local stakeholders in both case study areas noted that there is a strong focus on one general programme (the Jobs and Development Guarantee), which makes it difficult to handle a diverse range of problems locally. Instead, stakeholders would like to see a more diversified menu of activities available at the employment service. If there was more flexibility within the employment service, it could adjust programmes to the local situation. However, this could have a negative impact on encouraging mobility of the unemployed, which is a national priority.

For vocational education and training, the perception is that financial resources are insufficient. In both case study areas, there is an acknowledgement that programmes are under-resourced when compared to the national average per capita funding. For higher education programmes, funding is based on national labour market priorities although there is some room to adjust the offering of courses to local and regional needs. The universities have large autonomy within the parameters of the national funding system. During interviews carried out for this project, stakeholders argued that there is generally an unmet demand for higher vocational education. Additionally, local stakeholders noted that there is an unmet demand for adult secondary education, especially when local governments do not offer a "second chance" to study for another diploma.

One particular challenge in Sweden is the difficulties involved in collaboration on the local level to offer joint programmes by the employment service and local governments. Restrictions on the employment service make it virtually impossible to co-fund programmes with local governments. With more flexibility and collaboration across organisational boundaries, the local supply of vocational education and training would most likely look different. On the other hand, the outsourcing of the services provides a large market for providers of training courses. The focus is on the specialisation of services, while critics argue that service integration would provide other benefits.

The staffing resources are perceived to be adequate for implementing the current workload effectively, but more staff would make the work of the employment service fully effective. The skills levels of staff are also perceived to be adequate but more training for staff could help to ensure that they have the appropriate knowledge and skills to fully assist clients. When it comes to outsourced services, the knowledge and skills levels of staff who will deliver local services are defined in the contracts.

Policy co-ordination, policy integration, and co-operation with other sectors

Collaboration between policy areas at the national, regional and local levels

Local actors involved in employment, skills and economic development policies meet regularly. Communication between employment and education/training actors takes place at least every three months through *Arbetsmarknadsrådet*, the skills platforms and local boards for specific programmes. Communication between employment and economic development actors takes place at least every three months through various partnerships and meetings by the regional development agencies, (Länsstyrelsen in Stockholm and Region Gävleborg in Gävle). Communication between education/training and economic development actors takes place at least every three months through various partnerships and collaborative networks. In addition, there are several networks organised by industry ("branschvis").

Considering the various forms of interaction, a general assessment is that the degree of policy integration between the policy areas of employment, skills and economic development is at the level where joint strategies are developed, including inputs from three or more sectors. The primary tool for this interaction is the regional economic development strategies and their more specific action plans. This is known as RUFS in Stockholm and RUS (formely RUP) in Gävleborg.

There has been a set of successful partnerships in the county of Gävleborg to take action against unemployment after the crises. Some partnerships were introduced by the central government in 2001 to handle the effects of the closing down of defence facilities in small towns with weak labour markets, such as Söderhamn, north from Gävle. Other partnerships were introduced to handle job reductions in large industries like car manufacturing in the southern part of the country. In 2013 a regional partnership was set up to handle the reduction of a major industry in the town of Hudiksvall, north from Gävle, with heavy involvement of the public sector and the social partners (see Box 3.1 below).

Box 3.1. **The partnership for Hudiksvall**

The closing down of the Ericsson plant for fibre optics in Hudiksvall was one in a series of unfortunate events in a county which was hit by several closings and restructurings. It was obvious from the start that the loss of 318 jobs would have a significant impact on this small town. In response, the local government of Hudiksvall organised a regional partnership known as the group for strategic co-ordination to deliver a package of future-related actions ("*strategisk samordningsgrupp för Framtidspaket Hudiksvall*"). This group illustrates the commitment by a large number of organisations to help in various ways. Furthermore, the readiness to form the group shows the level of collaboration in this region.

Some of the members are leading politicians, in Hudiksvall (including the mayor), and the elected chairman of Region Gävleborg. One is the county prefect (landshövdingen), appointed by the government. The head of the local office of *Arbetsförmedlingen* is in the group, as well as the vice-chancellors of two universities and the head of the research corporation for what is known as the Fiber Optic Valley. The group also includes the head of business promotion in Hudiksvall, representatives of two unions and the national human resource director at Ericsson.

Box 3.1. **The partnership for Hudiksvall** *(cont.)*

The partnership worked with three ambitions. One was to take action within employment policy, to find new jobs. Another was to work with business development and innovation, to commercialise ideas developed by the staff of Ericsson. The third was to work with other companies which showed an interest in hiring the staff who risked being unemployed. There are specialized groups working with the first two tasks, as well as a group for the day to day co-ordination of actions across organisational boundaries.

Kompetensforum Gävleborg is a working group where employers participate on an industry basis (*branschvis*). There is talk about merging this group with the new skills-platform. There is a regional strategy known as a programme for competence (*Kompetensprogram*) for the county of Gävleborg 2014-20 (Region Gävleborg, 2014a).

Collaboration is easier where geographical boundaries coincide. The large regions of *Arbetsförmedlingen* mean that it is more complicated to co-ordinate with other local stakeholders, compared to when the employment service was organised at the regional level by county, similar to the regional development agencies. There have been initiatives to co-locate services by placing parts of *Arbetsförmedlingen* together with other agencies or education providers. An early example was called citizens' offices (*medborgarkontor*). Other examples were joint guidance counseling (*Infotek*) and joint facilities for the delivery of courses (*Lärcentrum*). *Arbetsförmedlingen* participates in several thematic partnerships or networks (e.g. on migration, homelessness, green growth), slightly more in Stockholm (three or more networks) than in Gävle (one or two thematic networks).

Due to the wide variety of services provided by *Arbetsförmedlingen*, a large number of services are in fact co-located (e.g. benefits payments, support with disabilities, access to active labour market policy). Examples of services which are not co-located are the ones provided mainly by local governments (e.g. support with transport and childcare).

In general, local collaboration among the public providers seems to be quite robust. This is especially the case among the national agencies. This includes the employment service and the RDA (*Länsstyrelsen*) in Stockholm. It is also the case in Gävle with the employment service and the local government of Gävle. These organisations seem to fit in terms of size and mission.

Collaboration with the private sector and area-based partnerships at local level

Collaboration with the employers is emphasized in the work processes used by the employment service. The new work processes see individuals and employers as two inter-related target groups. Work with one group makes *Arbetsförmedlingen* able to provide better services for the other. It communicates regularly with many large employers, more or less constantly. For Gävle alone, it had 1 900 contacts with firms in 2013.

Education and training organisations communicate regularly with employers. This will be further developed through the regional competence-platforms. The perception among stakeholders is that the companies are generally not very good at predicting their future needs of skills. The new needs are different from the available competences since traditional industries have moved or closed down. A joint project has been undertaken in Gävle to help companies develop methods for this.

Collaboration with the private sector takes place through a number of networks or partnerships. These area-based partnerships in place incorporate representatives for all of the following policy fields: employment, economic development, and skills. Examples are *Arbetsmarknadsråd, branschråd, partnerskap för tillväxt.*

Arbetsförmedlingen regularly attends meetings of area-based partnerships at the local level. It also leads meetings and actively implements actions and initiatives agreed in the partnerships, when there is a mandate in national regulations. In Stockholm, there is some competition among the relevant agencies in these partnerships. Adult/vocational training institutions regularly attend meetings. An example is the newly implemented skills (competence) platforms (see Box 3.2).

Box 3.2. **Competence platforms: Partnerships for skills development**

There have been many kinds of partnerships for skills development over the years, often introduced by the national government and linked to the regional branches of *Arbetsförmedlingen.* In 2010, the national government gave the Regional Development Agencies a mandate to set up new partnerships called Competence Platforms. This has become a key area for regional development policy, where the interests of employers, employees and the unemployed often overlap.

The background for the partnership was the abundance of programmes for skills development, funded by all levels of government. The national government funds skills development through its employment policy, social insurance policy, and higher education system. Regional and local governments fund secondary education in many forms, including several forms of non-traditional education for adults. Vocational training is part of all these programmes.

Interestingly the mandate for the competence platforms is vague and does not spell out if the purpose was co-ordinated planning or merely the exchange of information. They also did not include funding to attract participation in the partnerships. A more fundamental dilemma was the difficulty to plan for future skill needs. However, some of the platforms are carrying out interesting work across Sweden. For example, Region Skåne (the southernmost region in Sweden) uses its role as co-ordinator to bring various stakeholders together to work on specific forecasts. Over time this has developed into an informal secretariat organised around eight themes, co-ordinated by different participating organizations (Lindell 2013).

The Regional Development Agencies (Länsstyrelsen in Stockholm, Regionförbundet in Gävle) act as brokers who can facilitate joint action on barriers to labour market integration (e.g. availability of childcare, transportation) – but they have not so far achieved concrete changes to facilitate labour market integration. There is much talk about the needs for transportation in Stockholm as well as Gävle, but resources for new infrastructure are limited. The local governments also play a broker role, due to their responsibility for local development and the large set of services that are delivered by them.

During the case study interviews with local stakeholders, there was a general agreement that collaboration is dependent on leadership within local organisations. A large range of activities can be carried out when the organisations are represented by strong leaders, who see the joint benefits of collaboration. In other words, when the representatives are more risk-averse and focus on their own objectives, it is more difficult to establish collaboration. The role of leaders at all levels becomes important to make the fragmented local systems of job creation and skills development work effectively. This means that the system of local collaboration may be over-dependent on specific individuals locally.

Evidence based policy making

Swedish policies are generally based on a high level of data. The national budget sets out a framework where achievements are reported and the contribution of individual policies are discussed. Generally, there is comprehensive descriptive data available on programme participation and impacts.

Evaluations are carried out locally, regionally and nationally. There are many evaluation agencies, which undertake research which informs policy development processes. This includes evaluations of employment policies (IFAU), regional development policies (*Tillväxtanalys*), as well as agencies for the evaluation of secondary (*Skolverket*) and tertiary education (formerly *Högskoleverket*, now *Kanslersämbetet*). Further evaluations are provided by the agency for public management (*Statskontoret*) and the national audit office (*Riksrevisionen*). The institute for future studies (*Institutet för framtidsstudier*) carries out a number of evaluations, as well as the Ministry of Finance's expert group on the public economy (ESO).

Box 3.3. **IFAU, the institute for evaluation of labour market policy**

The institute was one of the first agencies set up for specialized evaluation of a particular policy area. Now there are many such agencies in Sweden, providing independent analysis of particular policy fields and the actions taken (or not taken) by the government. The name, the working methods and the co-location at Uppsala University indicate that IFAU is expected to work with high academic standards. It has a scientific advisory board as well as an advisory group of social partners, ministries and agencies.

IFAU has a strong reputation and provides authoritative positions on several issues where it places great emphasis on developing quantitative methods of evaluation. Academically, the link to the Department of Economics at Uppsala University is strong. IFAU funds research by other researchers and encourages non-Economists to apply for funding.

There are 16 themes of research, and several studies relate to skills development, at-risk groups and the work methods of *Arbetsförmedlingen*. One recent study shows the benefit of skills development for single mothers. Another study, based on data from Denmark, shows how the efforts of the staff of the employment service make a difference to the unemployed when it comes to finding a job.

The local programmes and strategies refer to a broad range of locally specific data (over five indicators). Data is available for most indicators within the last one to three years. Regular surveys or assessments are carried out to ascertain the types of skills available within the local population. This is done by industry organisations (*branschorganisationer*), especially in ICT and through surveys by the unions and others.

Regular (e.g. annual) local surveys are carried out as to employer skills gaps and shortages. This feeds into employment and training programmes. Evaluation data is used and is regularly referred to in policies and programmes.

Ability to collect data and administer policies within travel to work areas

The travel to work areas (*arbetsmarknadsområde*) are constructed statistically by identifying the strongest patterns of commuting. Most Swedish regions (counties) now consist of just a few such areas, indicating that the cities are integrated with the surrounding areas. Commuting between major cities is also present, in relation to metropolitan areas like Stockholm, but also across the cities in the southern, more populated part of the country. Proponents of high-speed railways see them as instruments for further integration of labour markets, which improves employment opportunities.

There is some fit between administrative boundaries (counties) and the local travel to work area. The main exception in Stockholm is the city of Uppsala, which is in another county. All the counties surrounding Stockholm and their major cities have links to Stockholm, while only Uppsala shows up as statistically significant to form an integrated travel to work area with Stockholm. The links to Stockholm are generally stronger than the links between the surrounding counties. The regions of *Arbetsförmedlingen* divide this area into three separate parts; the city, the northern surroundings and the southern surroundings.

For Gävle, the main exception is the small town of Älvkarleby, which is in the Uppsala county to the south of Gävle but situated close to the southern industries of Gävleborg county. The northern part of the county is integrated with Sundsvall in Västernorrland county. The local government of Älvkarleby participates in one of the two sub-regional constellations (Gästrikerådet).

There is a good set of data for the local travel to work area, compiled by *Arbetsförmedlingen* as well as by Statistics Sweden (SCB) in collaboration with the regional development agencies. There is sporadic joint working with other local administrative areas on strategies or programmes. The regional programmes (strategies) of the European Regional Development Fund are a prime example. Another is the informal co-ordination through the Lake Mälaren council (Mälardalsrådet).

Theme 2: Adding value through skills

Flexible training open to all in a broad range of sectors

The volume of courses available is rather high in most parts of Sweden. There is a sufficiently broad range of courses available locally so that students can choose whether to study locally or go elsewhere. An exception is when someone who has completed secondary school wants to go back to study another programme and the local government has restricted the access only to dropouts. This restricts the ability of an individual to pursue “second chance” learning for those who would like to change their career or skills after leaving secondary school.

The majority of training courses are affordable to the majority of local residents. All public courses are provided for free, but paying for living costs can be a challenge for some individuals, such as those supporting a family, even when the unemployment benefit is given to cover living expenses.

There are examples where the course sizes are not sufficient to accommodate demand. For example, training places available within the construction sector are sufficient however within the Stockholm region, stakeholders argue there is unmet demand for training places in information and communications technology (ICT). There

Figure 3.3. **Dashboard results: Adding value through skills**

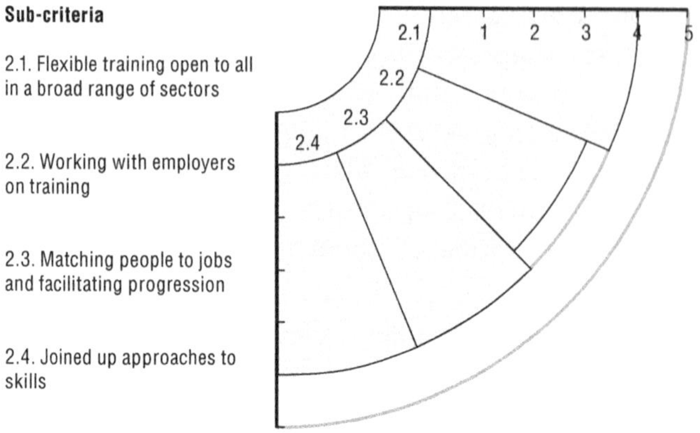

are also examples where the demand is lower than the supply of courses, such as the demand for education in the health care sector.

During the OECD study visit, local stakeholders highlighted how demand is dependent on cost (e.g. availability of subsidies). In other words, public funding and subsidies for certain training courses increases the demand for them. This is a logical observation about supply and demand, which is equivalent to saying that the future benefits are not high enough to motivate people to invest more in their skills development. Hence, there are more factors to take into consideration from an economic point of view, such as future salaries and the readiness to take risks.

Flexible short-term modular training is available in a wide variety of subject areas or sectors. As above, courses are affordable to the majority of local residents, while course sizes are sometimes not sufficient to accommodate demand. Vocational training is provided by *Arbetsförmedlingen* and by the local governments through Komvux. The majority of this training is certified – this includes the training provided through the higher vocational education pathway (*Yrkeshögskolan*). The training provided by Komvux is certified by being awarded a diploma (*betyg*).

After-hours training is available in many subject areas or sectors, which is affordable to the majority of local residents. Examples are courses at universities and Swedish for immigrants (SFI). A variety of courses are offered on evenings and weekends. Higher education is offered as outreach (distance) courses. Tuition is free, however living expenses can prevent access for some individuals.

Unemployed people and lower-skilled workers

Subsidised training (over six weeks in length) is available to the unemployed in a number of sectors. Many courses are primarily for the unemployed and require full-time studies. The employment service provides courses for those who have been unemployed for three months or longer. Courses for people with a job are either provided through the job training or on spare time, by individual effort. There are example of training being provided through European Social Fund projects, such as BraFöre, which aims to provide more courses for people with a job. Some industries (*branscher*) are involved in organising training as well as within the higher vocational education sector (*Yrkeshögskolan*).

Outreach programmes are in place to ensure that harder to reach groups access basic skills training. One example is providing education at boarding schools with non-traditional methods (*folkhögskola*) for young people. Another example is to provide courses in Swedish for illiterate immigrants (*analfabeter*). Some vocational training courses include support with developing higher level generic skills (including networking, communication, leadership, innovation and problem solving). These skills are generally provided whenever it is considered relevant. They are part of most courses delivered through *Yrkeshögskolan*.

Working with employers on training

There is a mixed picture when it comes to working with the employers. Higher vocational education (*Yrkeshögskolan*) is based on collaboration, where employers are responsible for on the job-training. During the OECD study visit, local stakeholders highlighted that funding for these types of programmes is limited to a number of employers and industries. Another initiative for collaboration with employers are so-called colleges in manufacturing and care. This aims to take a comprehensive and industry-driven view of postsecondary education needs.

When it comes to traditional education, employers often report problems with the training curriculum not being aligned to their needs/demand. Many universities are involved in cooperative programmes with employers, where the students get the chance to work for ten weeks with a company. This is particularly common among the programmes in business administration and engineering, which provide a major part of the workforce for private businesses.

It is estimated that more than 3% of average business turnover is invested in workforce training and skills development. There are specific programmes and initiatives in place to increase workplace training. Examples are found in the ICT sector in Stockholm as well as in a general effort to increase the on the job-training ("praktik"). There is a specific programme by *Arbetsförmedlingen* to provide such positions to unemployed youth. There are also employers' organisations and others who assist in recruiting interested companies as well as interested youth. The term *praktik* is used more broadly to cover all sorts of on the job-training. It can be paid, unpaid or with benefits such as subsidised student loans, if it is part of a programme in higher education. There can be additional subsidies for employers, for example in the apprenticeship system, where employers are expected to provide workbased learning. Without subsidies, it can be a form of cost-sharing with the companies, as in the higher vocational education system.

Dual training and apprenticeships

Apprenticeships (*lärlingsplatser*) have been discussed for a long time and have been introduced as an alternative to vocational secondary school. Apprenticeships are offered in a narrow range of sectors (e.g. including services), primarily the construction sector, and taken up by fewer than 20% of young people (age 15-24). There is nothing available that can be described as pre-apprenticeship training and support to broaden access.

A formal apprenticeship system was introduced recently, which provides training programmes for youth, including a mix of classroom and on-the-job training and instruction. It differs from the German or Austrian models by being shorter and not leading to unique occupations. This indicates that the Swedish model is not seen as an alternative training path, but rather a pragmatic way to introduce more young people to their first job. Hence, the debate on the risk that this becomes a means to find cheap labour, rather than a means to train labour for new types of occupations, as mentioned by some stakeholders.

Training customized to the needs of the employers is available in many sectors or generic skills areas. However, it is difficult to quickly develop new programmes by *Arbetsförmedlingen*, due to legal challenges of outsourcing decisions. It takes longer to decide on new programmes by Yrkeshögskolan, while Komvux is much more flexible in developing new programmes. Existing courses can be provided much quicker, within existing contracts.

Box 3.4. *Jobbtorg* by local governments for people without unemployment benefits.

Jobbtorg is literally a marketplace for jobs, where those out fo work get coaching and support as well as a chance to meet with prospective employers. It is run by local governments in association with *Arbetsförmedlingen*. The clients have to be registered as unemployed with *Arbetsförmedlingen*, while the services are organized entirely by the local governments who also pay the benefits for the unemployed. This is a service for youth, immigrants and other unemployed who are not eligible for unemployment benefits, for example because they have never had a first job.

The services provided are in coaching, matching and guidance counselling. In other words, it is about how to apply for a job and help in finding a job or education. In the city of Stockholm, these services are provided for about 6 000 clients a year, half of which were helped out of unemployment. There are seven offices in different parts of the city. One difference from *Arbetsförmedlingen* is that the entry into the service is through the case worker. All clients living on welfare benefits have a case worker as a contact, who arranges the first meeting together with the coach.

There is also a further service known as Jobbstart, where a client can get a training opportunity in a job-like situation. Here the client can work as a host or hostess in the city services for the elderly, the disabled or the maintenance of parks. The park service includes being a general host for visitors to Stockholm. It begins with a three week-training course, followed by a three month on the job-training ("praktik"). After this a person can be hired for a full year. 100 people yearly are offered the on the job-training and 50 people are hired. Jobbstart also provides further courses, job-training and job-testing. It organises more specialized services for people with more diverse backgrounds, for example social problems, drug abuse or previous convictions.

There are no matched funding/subsidies to help business to access courses. On the other hand, they are provided free of charge for the unemployed, which is also a kind of subsidy for firms in general. There is no particular support to stimulate skills development in SMEs. Companies are treated the same regardless of size. Larger companies and employers' associations generally do not actively support skills development in SMEs. The transport sector is an exception, as well as some franchises like food retailers ICA and McDonald's, which run in-house training programmes for their staff in business-related skills.

Matching people to jobs and facilitating progression

Secondary schools provide career advice (Studie- och yrkesvägledning, SYV) for their students. This advice is informed by a general knowledge of the local labour market. Through *Arbetsförmedlingen* as well as Komvux, a well-developed system of adult careers advice is available (both to employed and unemployed adults), informed by knowledge of the local labour market. This was formerly provided jointly in many places through the so-called Infotek. There are active attempts to link graduates to local industries for example through career fairs and work placements. *Arbetsmarknadsdagar* is a common concept where organisations and others provide an arena where information can be exchanged. Nationally, the fair by SACO is especially geared towards university education.

While Sweden comes from a tradition of few hierarchies, there is now work taking place to create career ladders to improve progression for low paid workers in some sectors. This is addressed by the European Social Fund. It is also in focus by LO, the major blue collar union. Mapping of job profiles by local sector/cluster extensively informs programming and careers advice. This is part of the work by *Arbetsförmedlingen*.

Box 3.5. **The European Social Fund in Sweden**

The European Social Fund is an instrument of the European Union to support skills development and to fight exclusion. It was set up in 1957 and has operated in Sweden since 1995, when Sweden became a member of the European Union. It is organized as a national agency (ESF-rådet) with the assignment to co-fund projects related to skills development for the employed and to fight exclusion. This selection of topics is based on the European framework regulation and the Swedish overall strategy for competitiveness, entrepreneurship and employment, which provides an integrated context for national policies (including regional and local) and European policies, including the operations of the European Regional Development Fund in Sweden.

In the first area ESF funds gap analyses and training programmes. It has helped a large number of small companies to measure available skills as well as the future need for skills. About a million people have received training since 1995. The programmes are co-funded by the ESF, which means that companies at least have to invest their time in the projects.

The second area is exclusion. The ESF co-funds projects, often with *Arbetsförmedlingen*, *Försäkringskassan* and the local governments, since they are the main providers of benefits for people who do not have a job. Many civil society organisations are involved as participants or managers of projects. The focus is very wide and covers situations from a first on the job-training to providing meaningful work for individuals with special needs.

The design of the ESF has recently been revised to increase the likelihood that primary agencies like *Arbetförmedlingen* and *Försäkringskassan* will benefit from the often innovative projects, to take advantage of new methods and to take a long-term perspective on the clients who have been in the projects. For 2014-20, the government emphasises collaboration with other agencies and the integration of employment and education policies.

Effective activation and job matching service

All unemployed people receive counselling within the first three months. This is a key point in Swedish active labour market policy. During the first three months, the focus is mainly on those who are at the risk of long-term unemployment. Other clients are expected to find work on their own for the first three months. This means that less than 25% of the registered unemployed receive training or work experience within the first three months of their unemployment claim.

There are no regional/local strategies in place at *Arbetsförmedlingen* to better match skills supply and demand, but these issues are part of the regional development planning and collaboration in most regions. Employment policies focus on national matching and explicitly warn against unnecessarily changing jobs.

There is no incentive for ensuring the sustainability of job matches by the employment service to ensure that jobs are quality jobs. The policy is that short-term jobs are better than no jobs. All job offers can be published in the data bank, but some are not taken into account by the staff, for example if the jobs are short-term or without a guaranteed salary. *Arbetsförmedlingen* monitors their former clients to see how many hold a job or are in training programmes after 90 days.

Options exist for validating informally acquired skills in a broad range of sectors. *Arbetsförmedlingen* provides such a validation service called *yrkeskompetensbedömning*. Here, the unemployed can work for a limited time with certified employers who will make a judgement (validation) of the skills possessed by the individual.

Joined up approaches to skills

A range of specific actions have been taken in order to retain or attract talent. All levels of government take actions to attract foreign companies through promotion of inward investment, often together with the promotion of tourism. Many local governments invest in culture to make their cities attractive.

A local co-ordinated approach to skills and talent development has been developed and implemented in most parts of the country, involving several different policy sectors (including employment, skills and economic development). This is one of the common themes of regional development collaboration. Skills development is often addressed in the regional plans (RUS/RUFS). It is also the focus of the skills platforms and the remaining older partnerships like *Arbetsmarknadsrådet* and *Kompetensrådet*.

Regional strategies for skills development and the development of "competence" have been put in place to provide a foundation for the new regional design of the European Social Fund from 1 July 2014. The idea is that every region should have a strategy which can be used to integrate investments in skills development by European, national, regional and local funding. This strategy should be linked to the overall strategy for the region (RUS/RUFS). It is expected that *Arbetsförmedlingen* can collaborate within these planning frameworks as far as collaboration is compatible with the national goals of the employment policy.

The competence programme for Gävleborg has a wide definition of competence, covering prerequisites for learning as well as more traditional skills development (Region Gävleborg 2014a). The prerequisites are mainly about the influence on one's personal situation and on the development of society. In this section, the region focuses on getting to people to vote, getting the local governments to adopt strategies for the inclusion of youth and making education support entrepreneurship.

The section on skills development has targets for things like the completion of secondary school, the amount of tertiary education, validation of acquired competencies and closer co-operation by schools with work (*arbetslivet*). A final section addresses the need for skills development for the employed as well as collaboration by education providers with employers.

Theme 3: Targeting policy to local employment sectors and investing in quality jobs

Figure 3.4. **Dashboard results: Targeting policy to local employment sectors and investing in quality jobs**

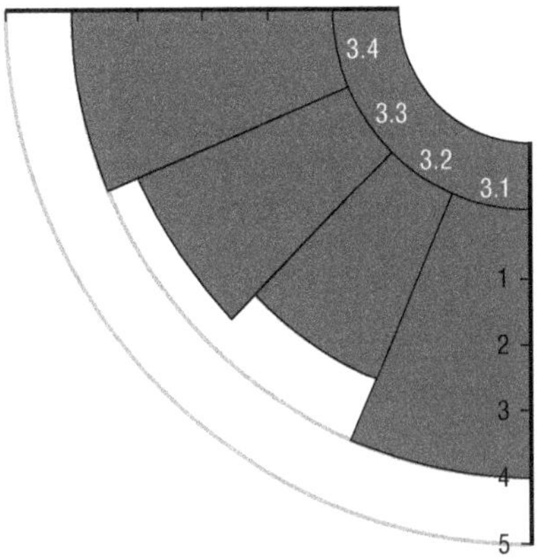

Relevance of provision to important local employment sectors and global trends and challenges

Employment programmes and initiatives are geared to important local employment sectors by *Arbetsförmedlingen*. Analysis has also been carried out by regional development agencies in collaboration with other organisations to inform a broad range of employment programmes. This has been part of regional development policy in most regions, through the overall planning documents (RUS, RUFS) or through the partnerships for skills development (e.g. *Arbetsmarknadsrådet*).

There are many overviews of the clusters in the wider Stockholm area available (OECD, 2006). However, the strategy for the Stockholm county (RUFS) is careful not to make claims on where the future jobs will be. The biotech cluster has taken a hit when Astra Zeneca decided to move their research away from Södertälje. Nevertheless, all levels of government have taken actions to improve the attractiveness of the remaining companies and the universities to ensure that the cluster remains world-class. Similarly, the ICT-cluster based in Kista has suffered when Ericsson has lost market-share in telecommunications. In spite of these events, there is still a need to find skilled labour at many levels, from top researchers to engineers and skilled workers for the factories producing pharmaceuticals. These industries in turn require services of various kinds, from logistics to financial services, which creates further demand for skilled labour.

The strategy (RUFS) has an action plan for a region of knowledge, which looks primarily at the supply of university graduates and stimulates collaboration among higher education institutions in the wider area. It identifies bottlenecks such as a shortage of student housing. As a background it states that there is already successful collaboration in the region on vocational education and other forms of skills development.

Each of the clusters are supported by business organisations. For example, Stockholm IT Region is an organisation set up by companies and public organisations to support the development of the Stockholm ICT-cluster. It works on international marketing and competence development. The inflow of skilled labour is an important prerequisite for the development of the cluster.

The strategy for the county of Gävleborg (RUS) is also careful not to make strong projections. Its annex on innovation and industry highlights the two traditional areas of strength, pulp and paper as well as steel. It furthermore points to the new clusters which have been promoted by all levels of government to diversify the industrial base. One is the previously mentioned Fiber Optic Valley. Another is Triple Steelix (a play on "triple helix", as a formula for collaboration among companies, universities and the public sector, which in turn is a play on "double helix", the design of the DNA-molecule). Other initiatives are related to ICT and the development of tourism.

The previously mentioned strategy on competence for Gävleborg is at a high level of abstraction, indicating targets which need to be broken down into activities. It is connected to a well-developed arena for collaboration, the forum for competence, which stimulates collaboration on competence development at all levels of education and training, regionally as well as locally.

The level of detail in the regional plans for competence development has generally varied according to the size of the region as well as the diversification of the industry and the level of collaboration. Sometimes the focus is on understanding the underlying trends, as in the competence platforms in Skåne. At other times, the focus is on meeting urgent and identifiable needs. One example is the programme in Stockholm to support the ICT-cluster through skills development. Another example was in the region of Östergötland, where there was at one time an agreement by the education providers to focus on nurses and mid-range engineers, based on a gap-analysis for the region.

Analysis has been carried out, regarding employment programmes on how emerging global trends might impact on the local labour market. This has led to an interest in working with new specialties such as developers of computer games and the recruitment of soldiers for the Swedish defense forces, as well as with the foreseen increasing need for skilled labour in health care. A caveat is that, as previously mentioned, employment policies and programmes in Sweden emphasise mobility and only support local needs if there is a shortage of skills in a particular sector. In other words, reskilling is undertaken if the person wants to move into an area of shortage ("bristyrke"), but not if the person wants to move out of an area where there is a shortage of skilled people.

For adult education and vocational training, the Yrkeshögskolan programmes are delivered by a limited time (two years) so they can be responsive to demands in the labour market, which are local, regional, national, or global. Programmes are terminated and new programmes are introduced every year to ensure the system is responsive to employer demands and the labour market.

Work with employers on skills utilisation and productivity

Skills utilisation and productivity

Skills utilisation approaches look at how the workforce is structured and the relationship between an individual's skills and the needs of business. Skills utilisation approaches focus on how well employers are utilising the skills of their employees, which can improve productivity and profitability. Individuals also gain from the better utilisation of their skills through greater job satisfaction and autonomy. This approach avoids supply-side or "provider driven" training solutions, which may not address the breadth of an enterprise's organisational context. Instead, providers are encouraged to take on a workforce development role (Froy, Giguère and Meghnagi, 2012).

The internal organisation of work and the utilisation of skills is often considered the responsibility of the private sector and public sector employers. There is no public sector involvement locally or regionally in improving skills utilisation or work organisation. However, these issues have been part of the national tradition of research into work-life issues, now promoted by the agency for innovation systems, *Vinnova*, *Verket* for innovations system. There is also a project funded by the European Regional Development Fund which includes measures to promote the use of lean work methods.

However, local universities and/or colleges are actively involved in delivering and supporting applied research in a broad range of fields of relevance for the local economy. The applied research has partly been targeted to support local firms. The universities and colleges are not funded to do these things regularly but are involved with local firms in contract-based research. It is a Swedish policy that universities, rather than specialised research institutes, should do applied research to help private and public employers develop their products or work processes. This ranges from the development of new engines for cars to consulting on how to write a business plan.

The large interaction between companies and students in areas like business administration and engineering is providing firms with skills and some influence on their work processes, while the students and teachers learn about the firms. It is often said that hands-on experience with students is the best way to convince SME's that they need a university graduate who can restructure the way the company is doing business.

Box 3.6. **BraFöre: A project for skills development and business development**

BraFöre was a recently finished project to help firms and their employees remain competitive. The project is an example of an innovative approach to skills development and skills utilization, to meet a need for upgrading in the region of Gävleborg. It is one of many projects co-funded by the European Social Fund, which aims to support firms and employees, primarily through skills development.

The project started three years ago and has worked with 142 companies, where it has provided training for 3 450 employees, after investigating 12 000 individual needs. Skills development is a large part of the project, but it has also had an ambition to influence work methods in the participating companies. Part of the methodology was to work closely with industry associations in five industries of importance in the region: pulp and paper, steel, cleantech, ICT and tourism.

The project targeted SME's, based on the observation that they often find it difficult to estimate their future needs for skills. Hence, a key activity was to investigate skills gaps as a foundation for investments in education and training. The project was based on the experiences of working for a number of years with employees who face the risk of unemployment, where skills development can be important for the individual to find new work, as well as for companies to remain competitive.

Promotion of skills for entrepreneurship

Entrepreneurship has been a theme in the Swedish education sector since the 1990s. It is part of the curriculum and there is a lot of information available for schools, often provided by business organisations. There have been many projects to fund innovative methods for the promotion of entrepreneurship and making students interested in starting their own companies. Comprehensive approaches are taken to encourage entrepreneurship in public employment programmes. There are specifically designed employment programmes to encourage entrepreneurship.

For adults, there are support centres, such as *Nyföretagarcentrum* and *Drivhuset*. The subsidy given by *Arbetsförmedlingen* for the start of new businesses is the largest support of this kind in Sweden, given to almost 100 000 individuals annually. Here the main subsidy is to stay on the unemployment benefit for up to six months after the company is started. *Arbetsförmedlingen* provides support with issues related to the specific company, such as advice on the business plan, specific training or covering some start-up costs. The client can get support from other agencies and organisations specialised in helping business start-ups. *Arbetsförmedlingen* can give further support to cover extra costs for people with disabilities.

It is common practice for students to be offered training in entrepreneurship whilst at university as an additional option and partly integrated within the course structure. All universities have centers to promote entrepreneurship among students and staff. Many also teach courses on entrepreneurship. In secondary schools it is common to work jointly with the association for young entrepreneurs (*Ung företagsamhet*), for example by setting up test-companies for all students.

Box 3.7. *Ung Företagsamhet* ("young entrepreneurs") companies in secondary schools

Ung Företagsamhet ("young entrepreneurs") is an independent organisation which promotes entrepreneurship in schools. Among its major partners are companies, business associations and the agency for schools (Skolverket). One of its programmes is to help students in secondary school set up their own companies, known as UF-companies. This is a programme where schools participate and students get the opportunity of a hands-on experience to start a small company.

The programme provides a simplified way to register a company and work with it for a year. It includes market research, developing a business plan, meeting an advisor and raising capital. At the end of the year an annual statement must be made. The most spectacular element is the showing of products at a local fair. It can also include things like the making of an advertising movie and an environmental plan for the company.

Almost 600 schools participate with more than 21 000 students. Together they have started almost 7 000 companies. More than 1 400 teachers participate and are helped by more than 7 300 business advisors. Since 1980, 279 000 students have participated. The organisation is based on the concept of Junior Achievement, which is an organisation started in the United States in 1919. The Swedish version was introduced by a businessman and a professor at Linköping University, who had come in contact with Junior Achievement in the US. They were joined by *Industriförbundet* in the founding of *Ung Företagsamhet*.

Economic development promotes quality jobs for local people

All levels of government are involved in attracting inward investment. Information is made available to all potential inward investors, which refers to issues such as local human capital, local education and training institutions and the skills of the local labour force. This is often organised jointly in special companies (see Box 3.8).

Box 3.8. **Stockholm Business Alliance**

Stockholm Business Alliance is a partnership set up to collaborate on attracting investments to the wider Stockholm area. The partners are 51 local governments in seven counties, not only in Stockholm county and its closest neighbours (Uppsala and Södermanland county), but also the counties to the west in the Lake Mälaren Council, Mälardalsrådet (Västmanland and Örebro counties) and two counties further north (Gävleborg and Dalarna). The partnership operates internationally under the slogan "Stockholm – Capital of Scandinavia".

In addition to pooling resources, the partners provide some local resources and also work with issues related to the promotion of the local business climate. One important issue in a welfare state like Sweden is how people with small businesses are treated by the providers of welfare services. It can be difficult for entrepreneurs to show that they work full time and have a need for full time child care, if the incomes fluctuate over the year. When access to child care is based on a documented need, it becomes difficult for people with irregular incomes to show this need. SBA tries to convince the local governments that it becomes difficult to attract new businesses if the entrepreneurs feel discriminated.

The Stockholm Business Alliance is linked to Stockholm Business Region, which is a public corporation owned by the City of Stockholm, set up to promote business development in Stockholm. It promotes tourism through the Stockholm Visitors Board and it supports companies. It helps individual companies handle necessary contacts in the local area. It also works with established companies to improve the working conditions for companies in Stockholm (*www.stockholmbusinessregion.se*).

It is standard practice to consider the quality of jobs on offer to local residents when making planning decisions in relation to potential inward investment. Some of the largest efforts have been made to attract high-tech companies, such as Pfizer to the greater Stockholm area. An example in Gävle is to attract more companies in the field of Geographical Information Systems (GIS), to support the local cluster.

There is now a discussion on the promotion of social values through procurement. While low price is generally the major consideration for tendering, it is increasingly common to ensure that local development and construction projects offer job and training opportunities to local residents. There are examples of procurement where the winner of the contract is expected to hire people who are far from the labour market, in phase three of the Job and Development Guarantee. The local government of Stockholm pays a subsidy to contractors to hire the unemployed for road construction. Ad-hoc actions are taken to ensure that public procurement requires sub-contractors to administer good human resource management (e.g. in meeting equality targets, local labour employed, training of staff). One example is the contract for food and cleaning by *Gävle kommun*, where contractors were asked to hire people at the risk of exclusion. Some contracts specify that apprenticeships should be provided. In addition, a broad cross sector strategy exists for supporting local employment growth and job creation (incorporating employment, skills and economic development actors). This is part of the regional development collaborative framework.

Theme 4: Being inclusive

Figure 3.5. **Dashboard results: Being inclusive**

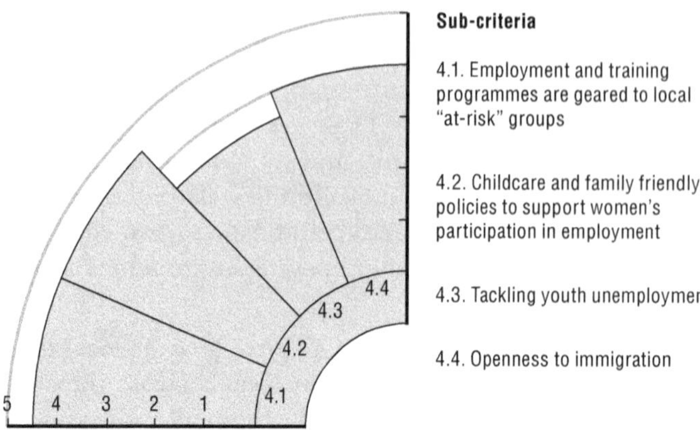

Employment and training programmes are geared to local "at-risk" groups

A broad range of those identified as at risk are served. This is evaluated and some progress has been made in reducing exclusion rates for these groups. There are many programmes by all levels of government which support individuals and townships (*stadsdelar*).

It is a priority for the employment service to help the long-term unemployed as well as those with disabilities. The employment service also works with local partners to create jobs/job placements for people not ready to enter formal employment (e.g. the disabled or disadvantaged). Comprehensive efforts are made, for example through subsidised employment opportunities or agreements with employers, to create jobs/job placements for people not ready to enter formal employment.

There is a wide range of subsidies which can be given for employers to hire people who would otherwise not find jobs, for example due to mental disabilities. It is also promoted through social enterprise (*socialt företagande*). Another example is the public company *Samhall* (meaning community) which provides shielded work and has yet managed to establish itself as a brand name. The public sector sometimes also play a leadership role – the Gävle local government has a policy that 1.5% of its employees should be individuals who are disadvantaged and would normally not find a job in the labour market.

The employment service participates consistently in area-based approaches to tackle places of deprivation. This is a big issue in large metropolitan centres, such as the Stockholm area, where large projects have been organized to support the city of Södertälje and areas in the northwest of Stockholm ("Järvalyftet"), where riots took place in the Summer 2013. In a smaller city like Gävle, the strategy is to target at risk-groups rather than specific townships. In reality, this means some attention for certain townships.

Specific training programmes have been provided for local at risk groups. There is vocational training specifically aimed at minority groups disadvantaged in the labour market. Vocational and adult training institutions participate in outreach activities. A broad range of training programmes are delivered through outreach directly into disadvantaged communities. Training in non-traditional forms, such as *folkbildning*, is well suited to work with a broad range of needs. One example is courses for immigrant women

Box 3.9. **Järvalyftet**

Järvalyftet is a largescale project to renew – uplift – a section of northern Stockholm where 60,000 people live. Järva is the name of the larger area, which is an old field with settlements for thousands of years. At one end is the extremely successful base of the ICT-cluster in Stockholm, Kista, where companies like Ericsson, Nokia and IBM are based. Next to it and along the other edges are housing areas with severe social problems, including the riots in the Summer of 2013.

The public housing around the field was built as part of the large-scale housing projects of the 1960s and 1970s. They have been heavily criticized for concentrating immigrants in pockets around the cities in Sweden, with a standardized offering which many Swedes try to avoid, hence leading to segregated living conditions in most big cities.

The basic idea of the project Järvalyftet is to take the opportunity to transform the area when needed maintenance work is carried out over the next twenty years. The new motorway around Stockholm will go nearby, which better connects the areas to other communities. Smaller houses will be added and small apartments will be integrated to open up for larger families to stay in the area and bring stability. New houses will look more attractive and the housing corporations are committed to providing good services. There will be investments in schools and supports to make it easier to start businesses. There is an ambition to take advantage of the cultural diversity, including the experience of starting companies in other countries (*http://bygg.stockholm.se/Alla-projekt/Jarvalyftet/*).

who would otherwise be locked-into the role of housewives, e.g. bicycling for Somali women, a project run in several cities to provide a first step towards skills development and introduction into Swedish society.

Vocational and adult training institutions participate consistently in area-based approaches to tackle places of deprivation. They are regularly part of the projects organised to support groups and/or areas. Furthermore, there is ad-hoc assistance to help people out of informal/illegal employment. One example in Stockholm is the joint effort by a number of agencies to tackle informal employment within taxi companies (*Samordningsgrupp taxi*).

Childcare and family friendly policies to support women's participation in employment

Childcare is well developed in Sweden. A very large proportion of Swedish children go to childcare of different forms. Most families can access affordable and subsidised childcare and it broadly meets demand. Affordable early year's education is also broadly available. Childcare is regulated by the national government and funded by the local governments. There are many cooperatives, set up either by the staff or the parents, which run these facilities. The mix varies across the country and reflects political priorities as well as how much children there are in specific areas.

There is great diversity in Swedish child care. It is funded through fees and substantial local government subsidies. They are often run by the local governments while there is also a large sector of private providers, for-profit companies as well as non-profit providers, often owned by the staff or the parents ("co-operatives", a part of the social economy). The child care owned by the parents often require unpaid labour, such as maintenance, cleaning and fill-in when staff are away. This is thought to strengthen solidarity in the group of owners while also reducing the costs (i.e. enabling a higher staff ratio).

Box 3.10. **Experimentation in non-traditional forms of skills development**

Folkbildning is a non-traditional form of education and skills development which is now undergoing further evolution in a non-traditional direction. It started in the 1880s with students from Uppsala University who published introductions on the topics that were debated when Sweden was modernized. They also travelled the countryside and gave lectures on these topics. This lecturing evolved into evening schools ("studieförbund") set up by social movements and political parties to educate their followers, who often had a very short background in formal schooling. In modern days, these organizations have diversified into formal skills development as well as new forms of outreach activities for people who come from other cultures.

Courses in cycling and swimming are given in many parts of the country, by Arbetarnas Bildningsförbund, ABF. This is based on the observation that cycling is common as a means to get to work in Sweden but not in all other countries. To be unable to travel by bike can be a form of exclusion. To provide the training can be a way to reduce the risk of further exclusion (*www.liu.se/uv/lararrummet/venue/de-cyklande-somalierna?l=sv*).

Another branch of folkbildning are the non-traditional boarding schools, set up at about the same time and with inspiration from Denmark, which has a strong tradition of education for the public, partly in opposition to the traditional Swedish schools, which have developed from the church. These boarding schools are now used by *Arbetsförmedlingen* to provide a second chance for young people who find it difficult to develop their skills in a traditional school.

There are many child care facilities with a special profile, in art, music or outdoor activities. Some have educational profiles related (e.g. Waldorf, Montessori or Reggio Emilia). Some are open at night. The offerings differ by local government. Some local governments have promoted further variety and have also funded family-based systems such as the sharing of services in the homes or even a subsidy to parents staying at home.

Child care is regulated by the national government through a syllabus (läroplan för förskolan) with specified learning outcomes, which makes it a pre-school. The national government also sets a maximum fee for the parents. The national government also sets minimum standards of availability, for example saying that children with newborn sibblings (i.e. when the parents are on parental leave) are only guaranteed to stay three hours a day.

Additionally, there is a well-developed system of elderly care. Most families can access affordable and subsidized care for the elderly within three months of applying. The tradition is that elderly individuals are provided comprehensive caring service by local governments. However, care provided by individual families is also quite common due to cost pressures on local governments as well as skills shortages in the care sector.

Many employers support families, with extra subsidies or flexible work hours. Specific advice is available to employers on implementing family friendly policies (e.g. job rotation, flexible maternity and paternity leave, crèches on site, part time work, career breaks). Many of these issues are regulated by law *(Arbetsmiljölagen)* or by collective bargaining. There is a debate on whether women are held back due to their bigger involvement in the raising of their children.

Tackling youth unemployment

With high youth unemployment in Sweden, there is a debate on the long-term risk of "a lost generation". Youth unemployment is a difficult area for comparative statistics. It is dependent on definitions and methods, where Sweden seems to stick to the strictest measurements (Statistics Sweden, 2013). This applies to the measurement of the population (youth) as well as to the subcategory of unemployed youth. The population is in some countries estimated from available addresses, which is likely to miss some immigrant youth. The definition of programmes for the unemployed differs. The same goes for the classification of apprentices who look for other jobs, as well as for youth on student loans who look for a job. Many of these details are due to the way the labour market operates, which makes it difficult to agree on neutral statistics.

However, Statistics Sweden argues that these differences cannot explain the variety in youth unemployment. The differences have to be explained in terms of the design of policies across countries, for example pay for apprentices and student loans for holidays. Paid apprenticeships in Germany, Denmark and Austria, but not in Sweden or the Netherlands, rises the employment figure. When student loans are not given for the summer (as in Sweden), the incentives become stronger to find a job but it also increases unemployment.

Policies have been implemented in the form of cross sector programmes/initiatives/adaptation of mainstream services to support NEETs ("not in education, employment or training"), who are not registered as unemployed. One example is the project *Unga In*, where young people hired by the employment service find other young people at risk to talk them into education. They run a "job garage" where they meet the drop-outs in an informal way. *Unga In* operates in five locations, including both Stockholm and Gävle is a project to fight exclusion among the young. The name means "the young in", which is a catchy label for activities related to a group which is hard to reach. It targets drop-outs who are not in any official support systems. The ambition is to find them and make them motivated for jobs or education. The risk is that they would otherwise be permanently excluded, with severe consequences for themselves and for society in general.

The project is an outgrowth of a well-established organisation called *Fryshuset*, after the storage house ("the freezing house") where they are located in Stockholm. *Fryshuset* was set up with the intention to provide a space for young people who otherwise felt unwanted. It became a popular meeting place in Stockholm and helped many young people to a more meaningful life. Fryshuset is now a partner in the project, together with the city of Stockholm and the organisation Friends, which runs programmes in schools to prevent social conflicts (i.e. to promote friendliness). The project Unga In is owned by *Arbetsförmedlingen* and co-funded by the European Social Fund.

Some ad-hoc initiatives are in place to support school drop outs and to recognize skills and/or support young people back into education or into the labour market. One example is the programme by the employment service to support non-traditional education at "folkhögskola" (see the Box above.). Another example is the informal collaboration between the employment service and the local government of Gävle to take preventive action before the drop-out, for example by pointing out the benefits for youth of solving problems in schools rather than in the programmes offered by the employment service.

Box 3.11. Plug in: A Collaborative Project to Improve the Completion Rate in Swedish Upper Secondary Schools

Plug In is a Sweden-wide project to reduce by half the proportion of students who do not complete upper secondary school in four years – from 24 percent to 12 percent. The project operates at a number of levels. The Swedish Association of Local Authorities and Regions (SALAR), which represents the governmental, professional and employer-related interests of Sweden's municipalities and county councils, plays the lead national co-ordination role. SALAR's five participating regional councils translate the national objectives to the regional level, promote regional collaboration, and support the work of schools and municipalities. Finally, local, municipal, and/or school authorities are responsible for implementing the more than 100 initiatives and projects that comprise Plug In. The European Social Fund provides funding for the project, which is matched by the local municipalities.

Because of the decentralized nature of the project, there is no single Plug In model. Rather, regions, municipalities, and schools have taken various approaches. Some projects focus on improving processes and systems – for example, improving the transfer information about at-risk students when they start upper secondary school and improving IT systems to track students across schools. Other projects focus more on support to students, such as enhanced outreach to students who have dropped out or are at risk of dropping out, individualized coaching and mentoring, and study support.

For example, the Gothenburg region has a regional focus on expanding on municipalities' legal mandate to stay informed about people aged 16 to 20 who are not in upper secondary school. The project supports municipalities in moving beyond just tracking these young people to active engagement. Through municipal re-engagement centres or hubs, multi-skilled teams work with these young people to help them identify positive next steps in their lives. In addition to this region-wide focus, individual municipalities and schools have also developed their own individual projects, many of which complement existing support measures. One municipality in the region, Kungsbacka, has developed a comprehensive approach, having implemented projects that provide individualized additional support, flexible modes of learning, and support to students with mental health issues. It is also tackling non-completion in adult education colleges.

In the Västerbotten region, most of the seven participating municipalities are using "First Rooms" to provide individualized support to students with high rates of absence, those who have left school before completion, and those facing other barriers. First Rooms are full-time, but temporary programmes, that use an approach grounded in cognitive behavioural therapy to motivate students to return to their studies. They also offer study support and link students with other specialised supports. While this general model is common amongst most of the municipalities in the region, each implements it slightly differently. For example, in the only larger municipality in the region, Umeå, the First Room draws students from several schools and has its own separate location. In one of the small and remote municipalities in the region, one of the activities of the First Room is fishing. This activity takes advantage of the municipalities' rural location and gives the sole staff member of the First Room the opportunity to build relationships with the students and promote group cohesion.

Nationally, Plug In includes an explicit focus on collecting and disseminating knowledge and information about strategies to address the dropout problem. PlugInnovation, an online knowledge sharing platform, was developed specifically for this purpose. However,

Box 3.11. **Plug in: A Collaborative Project to Improve the Completion Rate in Swedish Upper Secondary Schools** *(cont.)*

because most of Plug In's interventions started in 2013, it is too early to determine the success of the various interventions being implemented locally and regionally. A number of evaluations are underway, including an internal evaluation of ten selected projects and two external evaluations (an outcomes-focused evaluation and a process-focused evaluation).

Source: Stromback, Thorsten (2014), Plug In: A Collaborative Project to Improve the Completion Rate in Swedish Upper Secondary Schools, Prepared for 10th Annual Meeting of the Forum on Partnerships and Local Governance.

Openness to immigration

A first problem for migrants is to have their skills recognized. There is a national service, provided by *Universitets- och Högskolerådet* (UHR), for those who want to enter tertiary education to have their background documents validated in terms of Swedish qualifications. In other words, local referrals are made to national schemes for recognizing qualifications acquired abroad.

There is also a service by the employment service where qualifications are recognized through *Yrkeskompetensbedömning* for Swedish as well as international skills acquired. Local assistance is given with recognizing informal and non-professional skills and competences acquired overseas but this is piecemeal and does not cover demand.

Arbetsförmedlingen provides a service to immigrants and others who have acquired skills but have no formal documents. It is known in Swedish as *yrkeskompetensbedömning* and it means that a person can work on probation for an employer. It can also be with an education provider who has an arrangement with an employer. The probation can be as short as one day and for as long as three months. The person will receive a document and may also be offered employment. The document can be used as the basis for an individual skills development plan by *Arbetsförmedlingen*.

Box 3.12. **Swedish for immigrants**

Swedish for immigrants (SFI) is a programme with a national curriculum, provided by local governments and other providers of education across the country. It offers specialised courses for people who have a vocational/professional education from another country, for example engineers, doctors and teachers. Here, the idea is to focus on the vocabulary which is relevant for the job.

There are also general courses in Swedish for general needs. These course are divided in categories depending on the background training of the participants. It ranges from courses for people who are illiterate ("analfabeter") to academics. The estimated time to complete an acceptable level of Swedish is from two semesters (one year), in the best cases, and upwards.

The courses are provided free of charge. Participants are not eligible for subsidized student loans, but they may retain unemployment benefits or welfare benefits from the local government (*www.stockholm.se/ForskolaSkola/Svenskundervisning-for-invandrare-sfi/*).

Special modular courses across a number of different sectors are available to help immigrants to top up and adapt their skills gained abroad. This is mainly done through training programmes offered by the employment service. Language training is available to all skills levels and meets local demand. Language training is available targeted to specific occupations (in a few sectors). The programme in Swedish for immigrants (SFI) is offered locally to specific groups, for example doctors, where the language requirement may be the only barrier for a job. This is also achieved through work-life practice (*praktik*).

References

Froy, F., S. Giguère and M. Meghnagi (2012), "Skills for Competitiveness: A Synthesis Report", *OECD Local Economic and Employment Development (LEED) Working Papers*, No. 2012/09, OECD Publishing, *http://dx.doi.org/10.1787/5k98xwskmvr6-en.*

Froy, F., S. Giguère and A. Hofer (eds.) (2009), "Designing Local Skills Strategies", *Local Economic and Employment Development (LEED)*, OECD Publishing, *http://dx.doi.org/10.1787/9789264066649-en.*

Lindell, C. (2013), "Kompetensplattformar i Skåne" (*Skills platforms in Skåne*) in Rakar, Fredrik and Tallberg, Pontus (eds): *Behövs regioner? (Should regions?)*, Stockholm: RegLab i samarbete med Sveriges Kommuner och Landsting, *http://webbutik.skl.se/bilder/artiklar/pdf/637-2370-4.pdf.*

OECD (2006), *OECD Territorial Reviews: Stockholm, Sverige 2006*, Stockholm County Council Office of Regional Planning and Urban Transportation, *http://dx.doi.org/10.1787/9789186574970-sv.*

Region Gävleborg (2013), Nya möjligheter – Regional utvecklingsstrategi (RUS) för Gävleborg 2013-2020 (*New opportunities – Regional Development Strategy for Gävleborg 2013-2020*).

Region Gävleborg (2014), Innovations- och näringslivsprogram 2014-2020 (*Innovation and business programmes 2014-2020*).

Region Gävleborg (2014), Kompetensprogram för Gävleborg 2014-202 (*Competence Programme Gävleborg 2014-202*).

Rothstein, B. (1994), Vad bör staten göra? (*What should government do?*), Stockholm: SNS Förlag.

Statistics Sweden (2013), Ungdomsarbetslöshet – jämförbarhet i statistiken mellan ett anta europeiska länder, Arbetsmarknads (*youth unemployment – comparability of statistics between the adoption of European countries*)- och utbildningsstatistik 2013:1, Stockholm.

Stockholms läns landsting (2010), Regional utvecklingsplan för Stockholmsregionen (*Regional Development Plan for the Stockholm*), *www.osteraker.se/download/18.1f86c0e614421c414ce9eb9/1396251560463/KS+2014-01-14,+%C3%84rende+9.pdf.*

Chapter 4

Towards an action plan for jobs in Sweden: Recommendations and best practices

Stimulating job creation at the local level requires integrated actions across employment, training, and economic development portfolios. Co-ordinated place-based policies can help workers find suitable jobs, while also contributing to demand by stimulating productivity. This requires flexible policy management frameworks, information, and integrated partnerships which leverage the efforts of local stakeholders. This chapter outlines the key recommendations emerging from the OECD review of local job creation policies in Sweden.

Better aligning programmes and policies to local economic development

Recommendation: Ensure better policy integration and coherence between employment, skills, and economic development actors by strengthening strategic governance structures at the local and regional level.

This review has examined the level of flexibility within the public employment service in Sweden. Employment policies in Sweden operate under a national system, which places an emphasis on the importance of mobility to reduce skills shortages. Relative to other OECD countries, the flexibility within the management of employment policies is low. The major organisational changes of the past decade within employment policies abolished the semi-independent regional boards. There are now rather tight rules and regulations for the employment service, through a strong centrally managed performance and budget management system.

Previous OECD research has highlighted the potential benefits of providing more flexibility for local employment and training organisations in the management of their programmes and services (Giguère, 2008). The Swedish policy of encouraging mobility conflicts with issues of local flexibility because under a more flexible system, communities would tend to introduce programmes, which try to retain individuals in their community. There are a comprehensive range of actors involved in the implementation of employment, skills, and economic development policies in Sweden. At the local level, it is critical that these actors join-up their efforts for more efficient outcomes.

Following the crisis, partnerships are a key governance tool to better connect the supply and demand of skills to ensure greater economic growth and productivity. Employment services need to collaborate locally with skills and economic development actors. This study has highlighted examples of local collaboration among agencies and local governments. However, collaboration can be ad hoc and would gain from setting up specific fora, such as the more strategic use of skills platforms. During the OECD study visit, it was clear that much of the current local collaboration is dependent on strong leadership within organisations, which leads to strong variability – it is strongly dependent on "who picks up the phone" and whether they are risk averse.

The Competence Platforms which were set up in 2010 filled a need to establish a regional governance structure, which could bring together employment, skills, and economic development actors. However, their primary role is information sharing and exchange. There is an opportunity for these platforms to have more strategic focus on regional development and skills. They could also be given more resources to attract participation from a broader range of local and regional stakeholders.

There is room for the employment services and area partnerships to strengthen horizontal collaboration, and to identify the effectiveness of activation and training and best practices at the local level. In particular, employment policies need to be better connected to social welfare. At the local level, employment and social welfare policies are managed by different organisations, which operate under different accountability regimes. The lack of policy coherence between these systems can create unintended consequences, which lead to sub-optimal interventions for individuals who require more intensive services, which include both income support and employment services. There is a need to further integrate these services across the ministries in order to give local actors a workable toolbox.

Local authorities and employment services could pool resources to target the hardest to reach who need significant investments before they can re-enter the labour market. The model of "social reporting" piloted in some local authorities in Sweden could motivate local authorities to take a sufficiently long term approach to dealing with the disadvantaged. Employment services could capitalise on these efforts and add their specific expertise on effective active labour market policies. The lack of resource intensive support for the hardest to reach seemed to be a key concern for local stakeholders, particularly in Gavle.

Recommendation: Transform regional partnerships into systems of learning which effectively promote evidence-based approaches to job creation, employment, and participation

Partnerships need to develop a long-term strategy if they are to work effectively and have a lasting effect. For area-based partnerships, this strategy must include a vision for the region focusing on the outcomes to be achieved, an action plan identifying short-term priorities, and co-ordinated work programmes including activities and measures that will contribute to the achievement of long-term outcomes. It is also necessary to develop a shared commitment to the implement the programme and arrangements for monitoring and reporting progress.

Information and evidence play a critical role in bringing local stakeholders together. Often, this can be the "glue" that enables local stakeholders to identify common issues facing their community. In order to build a strategic approach that is relevant to local conditions, it is essential to have a strong evidence base. Authoritative and updated skills profiles of local labour markets are important in framing providers' strategies and strengthening accountability and can also galvanise local actors into a common agenda for action when used well.

In Sweden, there is an opportunity to build formal partnerships, which act as learning systems and encourage local stakeholders to learn and think together about what works best locally. This would strengthen the capacity to analyse local data and create evidence based approaches to employment and skills. There were previously attempts at forming learning systems at the regional level. Such learning systems could play an important role in building more effective services for clients, as well as establishing the most effective tools and methods for encouraging local employment and economic development. However, these systems would only work well if the regional actors have an impact on policy.

Adding value through skills

Recommendation: Ensure the adult education training system provides flexible opportunities for all individuals to ensure employed individuals can upgrade their skills

Overall, Sweden has a robust system of vocational education, which is evident in the relatively high participation rates. There is a comprehensive range of programmes, which are highly accessible as programme costs are subsidised by the government. Adults who did not finish primary or secondary school, or would like to access higher education can participate in Komvux programmes, which are delivered by the municipal governments.

Higher Vocational Education (HVE) programmes have come about as a response to a real labour market need and their operations are in concert with employers and industry. *Yrkeshögskolan* appears to deliver innovative programmes which are flexible and responsive to employer demand. While these programmes are a dynamic skills upgrading tool that is well connected to the labour market and workplace, the current process of changing them every two years may impact their long-term sustainability.

The government should also keep in mind that, in many cases, employers' needs can be short-term, therefore it is critical that other partners, such as unions and the non-profit sector, are also involved in designing training programmes and that there is sufficient emphasis on equipping individuals with generic skills which will enable them to be more adaptable and resilient. Demand for generic skills is increasing in today's knowledge-based economy and it is not just those at the top of the employment ladder who need these skills. OECD research has shown that, increasingly, those involved in "routine-work" (e.g. salespeople) can bring benefits to employers by being able to solve problems and feedback information from their communication with customers (Froy and Giguère, 2010).

Another challenge with *Yrkeshögskolan* and the broader vocational education system relates to the lack of sufficient part-time or flexible learning opportunities for adults who are already employed. Previous OECD reviews have noted that while Sweden has one of the highest adult participation rates in non-formal education, it is unclear whether similar opportunities are available for those seeking a formal vocational postsecondary degree (OECD, 2012; OECD, 2013). For those individuals who do not wish to stop working, there may be a lack of opportunity to pursue "second chance" studies to change occupations or careers. Sweden could explore the greater use of e-learning or other flexible forms of learning for individuals who wish to balance continuing education with work obligations.

Box 4.1. **FÁS E-College in Ireland: Flexible responses to the skill needs of learners**

Online courses in the E-College, set up by FÁS, are designed to be a flexible response to the specific skill needs of job ready individuals who require training with certification to assist them to re-enter the labour market. Online courses are available free of charge to unemployed clients. Courses are also available, for a fee, to employed persons who wish to update their skills. These courses are delivered completely online and technical support is also provided. All FÁS online courses last for 14 weeks, but learners continue to have access to the course and materials for a further ten weeks (i.e. 24 weeks in total). Over 30 courses are available and course categories include Operating Systems, Networking and Technical Support, Software Development/Programming, Office Applications, Web Design/ Multimedia, and Soft Skills.

Learners are able to participate in blended learning courses in selected areas in the near future, which provide additional online tutor support and a range of online training with enhanced learner supports including telephone, email, E-tutor and instructor led workshops. Some courses may also include one to one, group mentoring, assignments or project work.

Source: OECD (2014), *Employment and Skills Strategies in Ireland*, OECD Reviews on Local Job Creation, OECD Publishing, Paris, *http://dx.doi.org/10.1787/9789264207912-en*.

Recommendation: Increase the engagement of employers (especially SMEs) with the employment and skills system through greater outreach efforts and targeted programmes

Available data indicate that Swedish employers spend relatively large amounts on skills development and training for the employed. Nevertheless, it is common for employers' organizations to express dissatisfaction with the lack of skills in many traditional sectors. This is phrased in more general terms as a question about the relevance of post-secondary education. Employers have a critical role to play in ensuring that the supply of skills meets demand. Therefore, it is important that the employment and training system develops clear, coherent, and efficient engagement strategies to receive employer input on the relevance of skills being produced by the system.

While employers are involved in the development of Higher Vocational Education programmes (e.g. Yrkeshögskolan), there is a need to ensure they are fully engaged within other educational pathways. Sweden could look to other OECD countries, such as Canada and the United States, where employers are actively involved in an advisory capacity with the training system. In the United States, community colleges can rapidly develop courses because they use industry representatives as trainers. Because these trainers are from industry, it also helps to ensure a good relationship with employers. In some cases, community colleges have created a separate branch of their institution from the part of the college which offers more traditional academic courses, in order to be agile to local needs.

Box 4.2. **Strengthening engagement with employers in Ontario, Canada**

In Ontario, Canada, Programme Advisory Committees (PACs) help to ensure that we are educating and training graduates with the right skills for current job markets. They also provide community colleges with an early "heads up" to capitalize on emerging trends and new technologies.

These committees, reporting through the president, are responsible to the Board of Governors, and play an instrumental role in the development of new programmes and the monitoring of existing programs. Programme advisory committees represent a critical resource in ensuring the relevancy and application of college programmes and meeting the needs of business and industry. Some of the primary responsibilities of PAC's are to:

- advise college staff in defining graduate profiles and programme learning outcomes;
- provide input into the development and evaluation of the curriculum;
- recommend and assist the College in developing new programmes of study by providing information on the needs of specific industries/professions or developments in the community;
- advise the College on the availability and suitability of community resources and industry support for work experience components of programmes (e.g. co-op, clinical experience, field placement, summer employment and/or apprenticeship), and assist in recruitment of the placements for students, where possible;
- provide input regarding community and industry trends that impact programme outcomes and placements;
- advise the College on suitability of resources such as facilities, laboratories and equipment as they relate to the learning process;

Box 4.2. **Strengthening engagement with employers in Ontario, Canada** *(cont.)*

- maintain an active public relations profile for the programme and the college within industry and the community and ensure there is an ongoing public awareness of current and emerging career opportunities;

Source: OECD (2014), *Employment and Skills Strategies in Canada*, OECD Reviews on Local Job Creation, OECD Publishing, Paris, *http://dx.doi.org/10.1787/9789264209374-en.*

Another issue in Sweden relates to the lack of specific employment and training programmes, which target small and medium-sized enterprises (SMEs). In many OECD countries, SMEs are the engines of job creation however they often face different and unique barriers to accessing the employment and skills system. SMEs should be encouraged to provide more up-skilling opportunities to their staff and target them specifically at lower-skilled workers, as it is higher skilled workers who tend to participate in these training opportunities. Employers and workers have a joint role to play in this by supporting a culture of workplace learning. It is important to build on good bottom up collaboration and networks that already exist. For example, in Northern Ireland, United Kingdom, the government established a Skills Solution Service, which consists of a small team of trained "skills advisers" who work with SMEs to provide them with advice on existing skills provision and assist in designing and brokering customised solutions for skills problems faced by employers.

Box 4.3. **Supporting SMEs in Korea**

In Korea, there are active networks of SMEs that form sectoral associations. These sectoral associations are connected to the local training institutions and arrange training for individuals. However, similar to other OECD countries, the challenge with skills training in SMEs is that employers are reluctant to provide training to their employees because of potential worker turnover. To offset such concerns among SMEs, the Ministry of Employment and Labour supports SMEs with training subsidies. For example, SMEs can be reimbursed 100% of the expenses whereas for large firms the upper limit is 80%.

Source: OECD (2014), *Employment and Skills Strategies in Korea*, OECD Reviews on Local Job Creation, OECD Publishing, Paris, *http://dx.doi.org/10.1787/9789264216563-en.*

Recommendation: Better link the supply and demand of skills through the use of career pathways/cluster models

A sensitive issue concerns the design of secondary education, where one side has argued that a high level of academic content should be mandatory for all, including the vocational programmes, in order to make individuals flexible over time. The other side has argued that schools need more diversification, and a greater separation of academic and vocational programmes to avoid drop-outs, especially among those who find an academic programme challenging.

There is career advice available, through the employment service, the local governments and individual schools, which is a best practice within the OECD. In many places across Sweden, these used to co-locate to provide "one door" for the clients. The joining-up is often driven by individual civil servants who see overlaps and common needs. It can be encouraged in the new skills platforms, but there are obstacles in the design of the silos.

In Sweden, schools should work more closely with the public employment service and education system to create clearer, simpler and more recognised pathways into vocational education and training. Career pathway approaches can be used to support young people moving into more vocationally specific careers and set out how this can be done by articulating the knowledge, skills and competencies to better connect education with work in an occupation. They should prioritise not only supporting the growth of these jobs but ensure in-work progression for individuals in them through further developing the career pathways and ladders already established. Whatever individuals' starting points, economic development should deliver quality jobs for local residents. Tracing pathways through the education and training system into such companies and their supply chains, ensuring they can access more of the direct and indirect employment being created and that there is mobility from entry level positions upwards within a company or sector is critical.

Box 4.4. **Career Pathways Approaches in the United States**

In California, the state community college system, in compliance with state legislation, has instituted a career pathways programme that allows high school students to take community college courses and receive credit toward degrees. At the core of this programme are articulation agreements between high schools and community colleges in which specific requirements and conditions are established. This allows students, while still in high school, to understand the requirements for various careers, and gives them the opportunity to begin preparing for those occupations before entering college.

Source: OECD (2014), *Employment and Skills Strategies in the United States*, OECD Reviews on Local Job Creation, OECD Publishing, Paris, *http://dx.doi.org/10.1787/9789264209398-en*.

Targeting policy to local employment sectors and investing in quality jobs

Recommendation: Emphasise the importance of better utilising skills within employment and training policies and consider the mandate of vocational education institutions to be more proactive in this area

There is an interest locally to encourage quality jobs and to attract new companies to local clusters, however, in Sweden, public agencies have played a limited role in working directly with employers on the better utilisation of skills. A key pillar of job quality is better utilising the skills of those already at work. This requires not only considering how skills are provided by the education and training system, but the extent to which employers develop and utilise skills in the production process. OECD research has shown that local public agencies can contribute to improving how skills are put to use by using a number of different policy instruments, such as incentives for employers to invest in new technology and the promotion of more effective forms of work organisation (Froy and Giguère, 2010). In many countries, it can be difficult for the public sector to advise business on productivity issues, as there is a "credibility" gap which needs to be filled before policy makers can successfully get involved in this area. To overcome this, it can help to work with intermediaries. Furthermore, the informal exchange of experience and knowledge can be most useful in encouraging employers to "raise their game" and increase their productivity (Froy and Giguère, 2010).

In the Rivera del Brenta industrial district in Northern Italy, a local employers association has helped to raise productivity and skills utilisation in local footwear firms, through tapping into international markets for high-quality, high-fashion, shoes. Through the association (ACRIB), firms have collaborated on a common marketing strategy, while also pooling investment in training provision and helping firms to collectively upgrade their product market strategies. The region traditionally hosted cottage-based shoe making industries which mainly employed low-skilled blue collar workers. However the area has now become a global centre for the production of shoes for brands such as Giorgio Armani, Louis Vuitton, Chanel, Prada and Christian Dior, and now significant numbers of local people are employed in design and commercial development (50% in design, 10% in commercial development and 40% in frontline production).

The privately-run local polytechnic, *Politecnico Calzaturiero* has played an important role, employing firm managers to train local workers and job seekers after hours, while also offering management training, and investing in research, innovation and technology transfer. The polytechnic therefore invests in skills supply whilst also optimising skills utilisation through new product development and improved human resource management. The fact that firms are members of ACRIB means that they are less worried about pooling training, technology and new innovations. Investment in local human capital will not only improve prospects for individual firms but also for the global brand as a whole (Destefanis, 2012). ACRIB has also worked in partnership with local unions to ensure that during this time, improved productivity resulted in higher wages and better health and safety for the workers.

The government in Sweden could consider how the public sector can be more pro-active in approaching small employers and advising them on staff training and wider human resource arrangements. This could include promoting knowledge sharing networks, and aiding incremental innovation. Public bodies could also encourage management participation in training, as better trained managers are likely to create more productive working environments for their staff. In parallel, companies need to be encouraged to make training and other skills development opportunities available to their employees. Advising on how to develop a quality-driven supply chain can also be useful to help local firms think longer term and therefore invest in increased productivity.

OECD research stresses the importance of not just building the supply of skills in a local economy but also ensuring that skills are effectively utilised by employers (Froy and Giguère, 2010; Froy, Giguère and Meghnagi, 2012). There are a number of tools which local stakeholders can use to support better work organisation and skills utilisation in order to increase productivity while improving job quality (see Box 4.5).

Recommendation: Consider the strategic use of public procurement in tackling disadvantage and promoting inclusive growth

In Sweden, the use of public procurement as a means of local economic development and to promote job quality should be more fully explored nationally and locally. While in many cases, it is part of the Job and Development Guarantee, there is potential to expand its strategic use in policy making and delivery. It is important to remember that the public sector can play an important role in helping to shape skills demand and utilisation locally, not only as a policy maker but also as a purchaser of services (Froy, Giguère and Meghnagi, 2012). National governments should ensure that the public sector at the local level has the necessary capacity to influence its local supply chain. This includes being able to require

Box 4.5. Tools to raise the quality of local jobs and improve skills utilisation

Guidance, facilitation and training

- Support technology transfer: facilitating investment in new technology by employers, setting up partnerships for the sharing of innovation and new technologies.
- Provide technical assistance to improve working conditions and work organisation and increase skills utilisation: this may mean increasing the discretion availability to f front-line positions in some sectors and encouraging a high level of active problem solving in the workplace. This can be a source of incremental innovation by firms, while also improving job satisfaction.
- Encourage participation in training for both managers and workers: better trained managers are likely to create more productive working environments for their staff. At the same time, companies need to be encouraged to make training and other skills development opportunities available to their employees. Providing staff with enough time to pass on skills and learning to each other is also important.

Influencing broader public policies

- Remove local disincentives to a focus on quality in the public sector: this may include changing incentive structures for local employment agencies so that they concentrate on the quality and not just the quantity of job-matches.
- Ensure that skills policies are embedded in economic development policies: local partnerships are needed between business and policy makers in the sphere of economic development, education and employment, in order to ensure that skills policies are understood in the context of broader economic development.

Source: Froy, F. and S. Giguère (2010), "Putting in Place Jobs that Last: A Guide to Rebuilding Quality Employment at Local Level", *OECD Local Economic and Employment Development (LEED) Working Papers*, 2010/13, OECD Publishing, Paris.

training, apprenticeship and employment opportunities for local people when putting construction, regeneration and other development activities out to tender. There are some Swedish examples, but public procurement can be further used as a strategic tool to meet wider objectives and can ensure that more public expenditure is focused on having a positive impact. The potential to use public procurement for inclusion, as well as wider social and economic goals, is being increasingly used in Wales, UK, through their "Community Benefits" approach (see Box 4.6).

Box 4.6. Using public procurement for economic, environmental and social benefits, Wales, UK

The Welsh Assembly Government has placed a strong focus on using public procurement processes to meet economic, social and environmental goals. By embedding sustainable development into public procurement, the Welsh government has recognised the role public procurement can play not only in meeting social goals, such as reducing poverty and social exclusion, but also the way in which it can be used to build strong, more economically successful local communities. The Community Benefits approach has been used to ensure that public contracts support SMEs and the social economy's involvement in public procurement processes, tackle long-term unemployment, promote equality, provide training, and ensure work meets minimum requirements.

Box 4.6. **Using public procurement for economic, environmental and social benefits, Wales, UK** *(cont.)*

An example of the positive impact of the Community Benefits approach can be found in the construction sector in Wales. Six (now completed) contracts worth GBP 146 million led to GBP 56 million in salaries to Welsh people and GBP 68 million spent in Welsh based businesses, some 82% of which were SMEs. Training and work experience were also provided to apprentices and disadvantaged individuals. The Welsh government has suggested that the very small fall in employment in the construction sector (0.4%) compared to other parts of the UK (up to 15%) is an outcome of the Community Benefits approach.

Source: Ministry of Business and Budget Wales (2010), *Community Benefits: Delivering Maximum Value for the Welsh Pound, Cardiff*; Ministry of Business and Budget Wales (2012), "Making Procurement Work for the Welsh Economy and Communities", Welsh Government.

Being inclusive

Recommendation: The government should continue to target employment and skills programmes to at-risk youth to develop their employability skills and better connect them with the labour market

Sweden's employment and training policies place a strong emphasis on the disadvantaged. In many OECD countries, skills are the great equalizer and a key route out of poverty. The economic crisis had a disproportionate impact on youth and there are risks of many youth becoming disengaged with the employment and skills system. As mentioned earlier, a key concern is the resource intensive support for people further from the labour market to deliver long term benefits. The current "work first" approach taken by the employment services may not be the optimal approach, even if it allows room for investment in education and training on an individual basis. Local authorities can help to deliver such an agenda if they partner with employment services to assist them with the technical aspects of effectively delivering active labour market policies and programmes.

While Sweden's youth unemployment rate is not high relative to other OECD countries, it is significant when looking at historical rates within Sweden. There are a comprehensive range of employment programmes that have been introduced in Sweden to assist at-risk groups as well specific areas of deprivation. The Unga-in project was a specific response that was introduced around the time of rioting within neighbourhoods in Stockholm in 2013. The government must continue to seek ways of empowering youth by giving them access to mentoring services and employment opportunities. Improving employability skills is also a priority. Investment should be made in early years education as generic skills are learnt early in life and not all children benefit equally from pre-school and school-age education. What is more, a growing evidence-base correlates the provision of quality early years services with longer term benefits for children from low-income and migrant groups, those most likely to be later classified as not in employment, education or training (NEET).

Box 4.7. **Pathways to Education, Canada**

The Pathways to Education Programme was created by Toronto's Regent Park community in 2001 and is now being delivered in 10 other Canadian communities. In 2001, 35% of Regent Park residents collected general welfare, 25% were on the Ontario Disabilities Support Plan

Box 4.7. **Pathways to Education, Canada** *(cont.)*

and 28% were employed. The average family income was $16 954 (compared to $25 593 for Toronto as a whole) and 56% of Regent Park youth dropped out of secondary school (compared to 29% for Toronto overall). About 80% of residents were visible minorities and Regent Park was home to a considerable number of new Canadians, 58% of whom were born outside of the country and spoke little or no English.

Recognizing that different factors come into play at different times and that young people often have complex lives, the Pathways Programme developed intense, multi-faceted and long-term supports. From the beginning, the Programme rigorously measured and evaluated both implementation and results in order to incorporate a culture of learning and continuous improvement. The Regent Park Pathways to Education Programme focuses on school attendance, academic achievement and credit accumulation, in combination with social supports like advocacy and mentoring. In partnership with parents, community agencies, volunteers, local school boards and secondary schools, Pathways provided four main types of support: academic, social, advocacy and financial. These have become the major pillars of a successful programme model.

Pathways' innovative, community-based programme has been helping youth in low-income communities stay in school and graduate to post-secondary for more than 10 years. Working in partnership with governments, social welfare agencies, and hundreds of diverse volunteers who share their talent and wisdom, Pathways is helping to break the cycle of poverty and enable strategic, long-term social change.

Pathways works alongside the school system, providing after-school tutoring, mentoring and financial assistance to address the barriers that can stand in the way of education. Each student benefits from a personal relationship with their Student/Parent Support Worker – part counsellor, advocate, confidante, social worker, and mediator – who motivates and guides students and their families, brings insight that can't be found on report cards, and holds students accountable to the contract they sign in order to participate in the program.

Embedded within trusted local organizations, and dedicated to equality, inclusion and accessibility, the programme is available to all students of high school age within the communities.

Source: OECD (2014), *Employment and Skills Strategies in Canada*, OECD Reviews on Local Job Creation, OECD Publishing, Paris, *http://dx.doi.org/10.1787/9789264209374-en*; *Pathways to Education Canada*, available at *www.pathwaystoeducation.ca/sites/default/files/pdf/Overview%2021_10_10.pdf*.

More could be done to promote entrepreneurship as a viable career option for youth. There is evidence that young people are enthusiastic about starting businesses (including non-profit) but they face greater barriers when starting a business due to lower levels of skills, less experience, more difficulty accessing financing, and less developed business networks. More should be done to support the acquisition of entrepreneurship skills by youth by embedding entrepreneurship teaching throughout the education system, providing information, advice, coaching and mentoring, facilitating access to financing, and offering support infrastructure for business start-up.

Box 4.8. **The Prince's Scottish Youth Business Trust (PSYBT)**

The PSYBT aims to take a balanced financial risk in supporting aspiring young business owners, reaching underserved young entrepreneurs. Most of the entrepreneurs need intensive support, and the coaching, training and mentoring provided is designed to complement each award of funding approved. The PSYBT provides:

- access to seed finance and early stage growth finance for young people starting and growing their own business;
- a transitional path for early stage micro-businesses, with a combination of financial products and wrap-around support designed to enable them to evolve to a stage where they are more able to access mainstream/other business finance;
- a pillar in a bridge for the excluded and long-term unemployed to help them back into the economy through viable self-employment;
- investment in local communities by facilitating the significant in-kind contribution of local business people and supporting the development of local socially motivated businesses.

Entry/selection requirements: Young people aged 18-25 years in Scotland who can demonstrate that they have the drive and determination to start and continue in business. The PSYBT is a lender of last resort and will only provide access to finance when other potential sources have been explored.

The PSYBT model of support stretches from pre-start advice and training through to post-start mentoring which can last for up to two years. The PSYBT model, combining micro-credit with a range of focused business development services, is a unique public-private sector partnership backed by the significant contribution of over 750 volunteers from local business communities. The support combines appropriate micro-loans with a range of business support services including training, coaching and ongoing mentoring. The PSYBT is a member of the Prince's Youth Business International (YBI), a global network of independent non-profit initiatives helping young people to start and grow their own business and create employment, currently active in 34 countries in all regions. The YBI develops and shares global good practice, systems and evidence.

Source: OECD LEED Policy Brief on youth Entrepreneurship.

References

Barr, J. et al. (2012), "Local Job Creation: How Employment and Training Agencies Can Help – The Labour Agency of the Autonomous Province of Trento, Italy", *OECD Local Economic and Employment Development (LEED) Working Papers*, No. 2012/17, OECD Publishing, *http://dx.doi.org/10.1787/5k919d0trlf6-en.*

Eddington, N. and P. Toner (2012), "Skills Formation Strategies in Queensland: A Skills Shortage?",*OECD Local Economic and Employment Development (LEED) Working Papers*, No. 2012/07, OECD Publishing, *http://dx.doi.org/10.1787/5k9b9mjdj4xr-en.*

Froy, F., S. Giguère and M. Meghnagi (2012), "Skills for Competitiveness: A Synthesis Report",*OECD Local Economic and Employment Development (LEED) Working Papers*, No. 2012/09, OECD Publishing, *http://dx.doi.org/10.1787/5k98xwskmvr6-en.*

Froy, F. and L. Pyne (2011), "Ensuring Labour Market Success for Ethnic Minority and Immigrant Youth", *OECD Local Economic and Employment Development (LEED) Working Papers*, No. 2011/09, OECD Publishing, *http://dx.doi.org/10.1787/5kg8g2l0547b-en.*

Froy, F., et al. (2011), "Building Flexibility and Accountability Into Local Employment Services: Synthesis of OECD Studies in Belgium, Canada, Denmark and the Netherlands", *OECD Local*

Economic and Employment Development (LEED) Working Papers, No. 2011/10, OECD Publishing, *http://dx.doi.org/10.1787/5kg3mkv3tr21-en*.

Froy, F. and S. Giguère (2010), "Putting in Place Jobs that Last: A Guide to Rebuilding Quality Employment at Local Level", *OECD Local Economic and Employment Development (LEED) Working Papers*, No. 2010/13, OECD Publishing, *http://dx.doi.org/10.1787/5km7jf7qtk9p-en*.

Froy, F., S. Giguère and A. Hofer (eds.) (2009), "Designing Local Skills Strategies", *Local Economic and Employment Development (LEED)*, OECD Publishing, *http://dx.doi.org/10.1787/9789264066649-en*.

Giguère, S. (ed.) (2008), "More Than Just Jobs: Workforce Development in a Skills-Based Economy", *Local Economic and Employment Development (LEED)*, OECD Publishing, *http://dx.doi.org/10.1787/9789264043282-en*.

OECD (2001), *Local Partnerships for Better Governance*, OECD Publishing, *http://dx.doi.org/10.1787/9789264189461-en*.

ORGANISATION FOR ECONOMIC CO-OPERATION AND DEVELOPMENT

The OECD is a unique forum where governments work together to address the economic, social and environmental challenges of globalisation. The OECD is also at the forefront of efforts to understand and to help governments respond to new developments and concerns, such as corporate governance, the information economy and the challenges of an ageing population. The Organisation provides a setting where governments can compare policy experiences, seek answers to common problems, identify good practice and work to co-ordinate domestic and international policies.

The OECD member countries are: Australia, Austria, Belgium, Canada, Chile, the Czech Republic, Denmark, Estonia, Finland, France, Germany, Greece, Hungary, Iceland, Ireland, Israel, Italy, Japan, Korea, Luxembourg, Mexico, the Netherlands, New Zealand, Norway, Poland, Portugal, the Slovak Republic, Slovenia, Spain, Sweden, Switzerland, Turkey, the United Kingdom and the United States. The European Union takes part in the work of the OECD.

OECD Publishing disseminates widely the results of the Organisation's statistics gathering and research on economic, social and environmental issues, as well as the conventions, guidelines and standards agreed by its members.

LOCAL ECONOMIC AND EMPLOYMENT DEVELOPMENT (LEED)

The OECD Programme on Local Economic and Employment Development (LEED) has advised governments and communities since 1982 on how to respond to economic change and tackle complex problems in a fast-changing world. Its mission is to contribute to the creation of more and better quality jobs through more effective policy implementation, innovative practices, stronger capacities and integrated strategies at the local level. LEED draws on a comparative analysis of experience from the five continents in fostering economic growth, employment and inclusion. For more information on the LEED Programme, please visit *www.oecd.org/cfe/leed*.

OECD PUBLISHING, 2, rue André-Pascal, 75775 PARIS CEDEX 16
(84 2015 05 1 P) ISBN 978-92-64-22863-4 – 2015-01

www.ingramcontent.com/pod-product-compliance
Lightning Source LLC
LaVergne TN
LVHW081421110826
845149LV00010B/1820